FOLK ART FRIENDS

FOLK ART FRIENDS

Hooked Rugs and Coordinating Quilts

Polly Minick & Laurie Simpson

Folk Art Friends:
Hooked Rugs and Coordinating Quilts
© 2003 by Polly Minick and Laurie Simpson

That Patchwork Place® is an
imprint of Martingale & Company®.

Martingale & Company
20205 144th Avenue NE
Woodinville, WA 98072-8478
www.martingale-pub.com

Credits

President ~ Nancy J. Martin
CEO ~ Daniel J. Martin
Publisher ~ Jane Hamada
Editorial Director ~ Mary V. Green
Managing Editor ~ Tina Cook
Technical Editor ~ Karen Costello Soltys
Copy Editor ~ Melissa Bryan
Editorial Assistant ~ Laurie Bevan
Design Director ~ Stan Green
Illustrator ~ Robin Strobel
Cover and Text Designer ~ Stan Green
Photographer ~ Brent Kane
   Photographs were taken at the home of
   Polly Minick on St. Simons Island, Georgia.

Mission Statement

Dedicated to providing quality products
and service to inspire creativity.

Printed in China
08 07 06 05 04 03   8 7 6 5 4 3 2 1

Library of Congress Cataloging-in-Publication Data

Minick, Polly.
   Folk art friends : hooked rugs and coordinating quilts
/ Polly Minick and Laurie Simpson.
       p. cm.
     ISBN 1-56477-471-6
   1. Rugs, Hooked—Patterns. 2. Hooking.
   3. Quilting. I. Simpson, Laurie.
   II. Title.
     TT850 .M55 2003
     746.7'4041—dc21

                                        2002156267

Contents

INTRODUCTION

After 35 years of collecting Americana, creating hand-hooked rugs, and making quilts, we decided it was high time to share our ideas and love of folk art in this collection of patterns called *Folk Art Friends*. As sisters, we've been friends for more years than we'd like to count! And while one of us doesn't sew a stitch, and the other doesn't hook, we find our art forms have a similar graphic and tactile appeal—and they complement one another perfectly in our homes. We've been sharing our ideas and projects with each other for years, even though we live over 1,000 miles apart. Since Laurie's quilts and Polly's rugs work together so nicely in each of our homes, we knew that combining quiltmaking and rug hooking in one book would be a natural fit, too.

In earlier years, quilting and rug hooking were essential for addressing the needs and comfort of Americans and others around the world. Today we're helping to transform activities that were once basic and fundamentally vital for existence into art forms that are functional and appreciated in current times. We feel that rug hooking and quilting represent the epitome of fiber art, and in this book we'll share our personal style, how-to techniques for both quilting and rug hooking, directions for 18 projects, and a wealth of beautiful photographs to inspire you to decorate your home with an array of quilts and rugs. We hope you find *Folk Art Friends* to be instructional, informative, and inspirational—whether you're a novice or an experienced fiber artist.

While folk art can take many shapes and forms, from primitive hand-painted furniture to old toys, pottery, textiles, and other collectibles, we're presenting our personal interpretation of folk-art quilts and rugs. You'll find that the items in our pairs of projects complement one another, yet have their own unique qualities. Sometimes our inspiration came from an antique quilt, such as in the Stars on Stripes projects starting on page 41. Other times, one of us had a notion we wanted to develop, such as Laurie's take on a 1930s appliqué dog quilt or Polly's desire to adapt the shapes from her Noah's ark toy collection into a rug. Then the other of us followed suit!

The point is, inspiration can come from anywhere, even the simplest items in everyday living, and you can easily adapt ideas to suit your own needs. We even include a Make It Yours rug at the end of the book to show you just how easily you can take your rug-hooking skills and run with them to create your own personal designs.

Our hope is that you come away with many rewards: the knowledge and confidence to make your own projects shine; creative ideas for decorating with rugs and quilts; and a newfound appreciation for both of these age-old crafts as important art forms for today.

Polly McKillen Minick

Laurie McKillen Simpson

FOLK ART STARS

"I based the Folk Art Stars rug on a star rug I made when I first started hooking. Laurie and I modified the original design to create our first pair of projects for this book."

—POLLY MINICK

"I love the colors in this design, and the addition of the appliqué border adds a bit of dramatic flair to the quilt."

—LAURIE SIMPSON

FOLK ART STARS QUILT

Finished quilt size: 51½" x 59½" • Finished block size: 8" x 8"

Materials

Yardages are based on 42"-wide fabric.

★ 12 to 15 fat quarters (18" x 20") in assorted colors (reds, blues, golds, greens, tans, rusts) for star block background and appliqués

★ 2 yds. of black fabric for border and binding

★ ¾ yd. of green plaid for bias stems and leaves

★ Approximately ¾ yd. of assorted black and navy scraps for appliqué stars

★ 4 yds. of backing fabric

★ 56" x 64" piece of batting

Cutting

All measurements include ¼"-wide seam allowances. Cutting for the appliqué pieces is described in the block instructions.

From the assorted fat quarters, cut:
   20 squares, 9" x 9"

From the black fabric, cut on the lengthwise grain:
   2 strips, 10" x 40½"
   2 strips, 10" x 51"

From the remaining black fabric, cut:
   6 strips, 2¼" x 42", for binding

Making the Star Blocks

You'll need 20 appliqué star blocks for this quilt. Use your favorite appliqué method, or refer to "Hand Appliqué" on page 113 and follow the appropriate instructions.

1. Prepare 20 black stars for appliqué, using the assorted black scraps and the large star pattern on page 14.

2. Center a star in each 9" x 9" square and appliqué in place. Trim each completed block to 8½" square, taking care to keep the stars more or less centered within the blocks.

Assembling the Quilt Top

1. Sew the blocks together in five rows of four blocks each. Press the seams in one direction for the first row, and in the opposite direction in the second row. Continue pressing the rows alternately in this manner.

2. Sew the five rows together, and press the quilt top.

3. Sew the 10" x 40½" border strips to the sides of the quilt top. Press the seams toward the border. Sew the 10" x 51" border strips to the top and bottom of the quilt top. Again, press the seams toward the border.

3. Starting at the top of the quilt, appliqué the two shorter branches, then the top section of the vine. Continue appliquéing the vine, always covering the raw edges at the end of one vine section with the new vine.

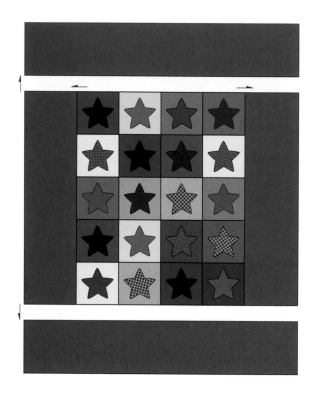

Beginning of second bias strip

End of first bias strip

Appliquéing the Vine

1. From the green plaid fabric, cut 14 bias strips, 1¼" wide, referring to "Bias Strips for Appliqué" on page 114. Save the remaining green plaid fabric for leaves. Your finished bias strips should measure ½" wide.

2. Referring to the placement diagram, right, and the quilt photograph on page 10, mark the placement of the vines on the quilt borders with a washable marking pen or pencil.

4. Use the patterns at right and on page 14 to cut six posies, four tulips, 13 small stars, four large stars, and two birds from the assorted fat quarter scraps. Cut 18 leaves from the green plaid fabric and green scraps from the fat quarters. Prepare the shapes for your favorite appliqué method and appliqué in place.

5. Make six yo-yos as described in "Yo-Yos" on page 115 and appliqué them to the centers of the flowers.

6. Use the pattern on page 15 to cut out and prepare one urn. Appliqué in place. Reverse appliqué the striped design of the urn. See page 115 in "Quiltmaking Basics" for details on this technique.

Finishing

1. Choose a quilting design and then follow the directions for marking the quilt top as described on page 116 in "Quiltmaking Basics."

2. From the backing fabric cut two pieces, 30" x 71". Remove the selvages and join the pieces to make a 59½" x 71" backing piece.

3. Center and layer the quilt top and batting over the backing; baste the layers together.

4. Quilt as desired.

5. Trim the batting and backing even with the edges of the quilt top. Use the 2¼" x 42" black strips to bind the quilt, referring to page 117 in "Quiltmaking Basics" as needed.

6. Make and attach a label to your quilt.

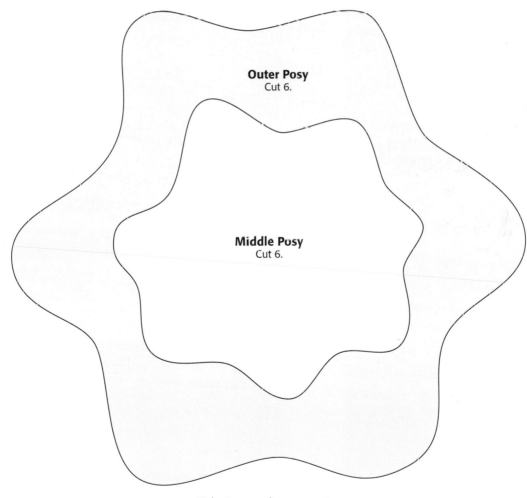

Outer Posy
Cut 6.

Middle Posy
Cut 6.

Make 6 yo-yos for posy centers.
Add seam allowances for hand appliqué.

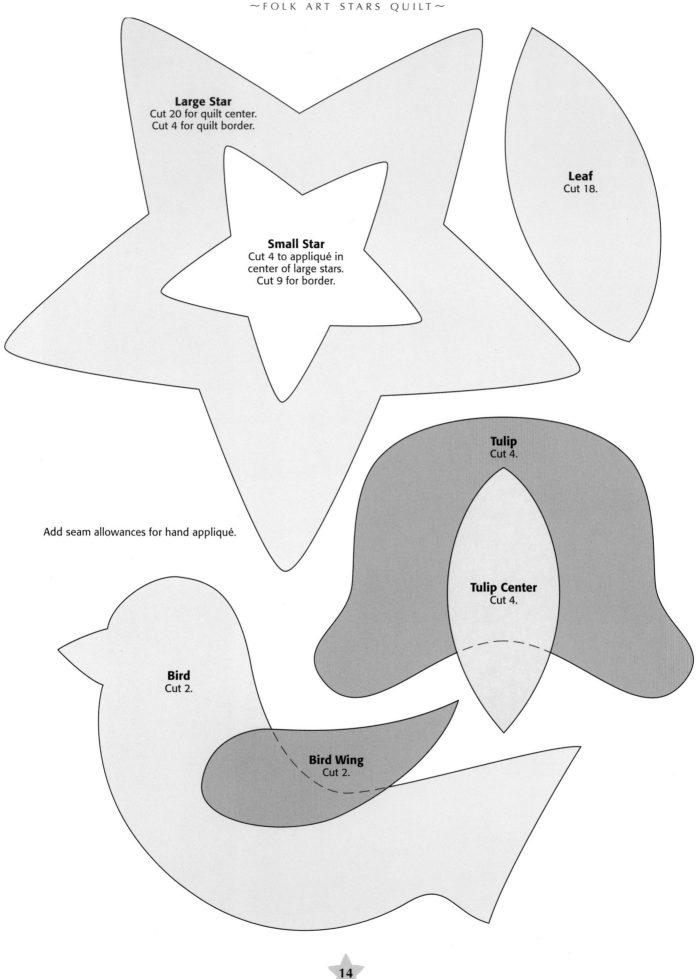

Large Star
Cut 20 for quilt center.
Cut 4 for quilt border.

Leaf
Cut 18.

Small Star
Cut 4 to appliqué in
center of large stars.
Cut 9 for border.

Tulip
Cut 4.

Tulip Center
Cut 4.

Add seam allowances for hand appliqué.

Bird
Cut 2.

Bird Wing
Cut 2.

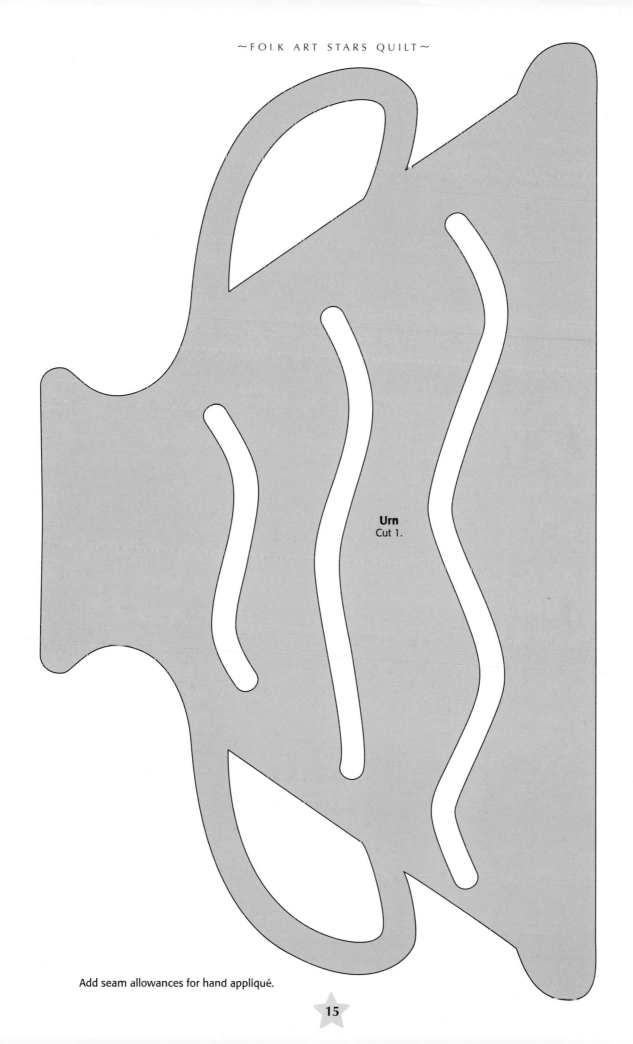

Urn
Cut 1.

Add seam allowances for hand appliqué.

Folk Art Stars Rug

Finished rug size: 38" x 45½"

Materials

Wool yardage amounts are estimated, based on 60"-wide fabric. (See "How Much Wool Do You Need?" on page 125 for more information on estimating yardage before beginning any project.)

★ 1½ to 2 yds. total of various shades of antique black for stars

★ ½ yd. of light color for corner backgrounds

★ ¼ yd. each of 20 colors for star backgrounds: mustard, blue, brick, red, green, khaki, gray, and tan. (If you wish to repeat a color, you'll need twice as much wool of that color.)

★ 48" x 60" piece of backing fabric*

★ 180" of binding tape for finishing

*If you use a hoop, add 8" to the backing measurements. See "Rug Backing" on page 122 for more information on fabric measuring techniques and backing options.

Cutting

Cut your wool into size #8 or #9 strips, referring to "Cutting the Strips" on page 125. I recommend not cutting all the wool at once as it is prone to tangle into worms. However, be sure to cut some strips of each of the various black shades so that you can mix them up for better texture as you hook each star.

Making the Rug

1. Transfer the design onto your backing fabric, using the pattern (which needs to be enlarged 600%) on page 132. For details on transferring patterns, see the directions on page 123 in "Rug Hooking Basics."

2. Outline and fill each star, including the four smaller stars in each corner, using the antique black wool.

3. Hook single rows of loops to create the black outlines that separate the colored squares.

4. Fill the background areas around each star using the various colored wools.

5. Create the border. Each stripe consists of three rows of one of the colors used for the star backgrounds. Change colors randomly for a casual look, referring to the rug photograph, opposite.

6. Hook the backgrounds of the corner stars using the same color in each square.

Finishing

1. Finish your rug using binding tape. (For tips on tape application and other finishing options, see "Finishing Your Rug" on page 130.)

2. Steam and block the rug, referring to "Blocking" on page 130.

3. Sew on an identification tag, referring to "Signing Your Rug" on page 131 for various options.

HEART PENNY RUG

"Nothing ever went to waste in grandmother's day!
Wool scraps were used to make penny rugs.
Large rugs were placed on the floor, but the
small, irregular-shaped ones such as this
were used for tabletop decoration."

—LAURIE SIMPSON

Heart Penny Rug

Finished rug size: 26" x 26"

Materials

- ♥ ¾ yd. of red-and-black plaid felted wool for hearts and tongues (See tip below.)
- ♥ ⅝ yd. of red plaid felted wool for background and backing
- ♥ ½ yd. of solid red felted wool for hearts
- ♥ 2 skeins of black embroidery floss

Cutting

The A, B, C, and D heart patterns are on page 23. They need to be enlarged 200%. The A, B, and C patterns also need to be flipped along the dotted line so that you can complete the full pattern. Do not add seam allowances for wool appliqué.

From the red plaid wool, cut:
    2 squares, 19" x 19"

From the solid red wool, cut:
    1 of heart B
    24 of heart D

From the red-and-black plaid wool, cut:
    1 of heart A
    1 of heart C
    24 tongues

FELTING WOOL

Unlike the wool used for rug hooking, wool for penny rugs should be felted before stitching. Wash and dry the wool using hot water and agitation in the washing machine and high heat in the dryer to more tightly bind and condense the fibers. This process reduces or eliminates raveling and creates felted wool.

Making the Penny Rug

1. Center heart C on one of the 19" squares. Using two strands of black embroidery floss, appliqué the heart using a blanket stitch (see page 116 in "Quiltmaking Basics").

2. Appliqué the small heart A onto the center of heart B, and then appliqué them onto the center of heart C.

3. Appliqué a heart D onto the center of each tongue.

4. Using two strands of embroidery floss, blanket stitch around the curved sides of each tongue. Do not stitch along the flat side.

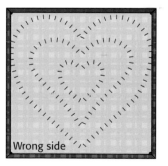

5. Using the wool setting on your iron, press under a ½"-wide seam allowance on each side of the rug front. To reduce bulk where the corners overlap, you can clip out some of the excess wool, if desired.

Wrong side

Turn under ½" and press.

6. Place six tongues along one edge of the rug's underside. Whipstitch into place on the seam allowance. Take care that the stitches do not go through to the front of the rug. Repeat on each side.

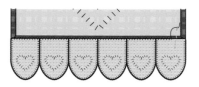

7. From the front of the rug, pin the seam allowance in place, as shown at right, with the tongues hanging outside the rug.

8. Press under ½" from the edges of the remaining 19" square of wool. Pin this backing piece to the rug front, wrong sides together. Whipstitch the edges together from the back of the rug.

A miniature Noah's ark perches on the Heart penny rug. The ark is one of the earliest in Polly's collection, and although it's not blue like most of the others, how could she resist?

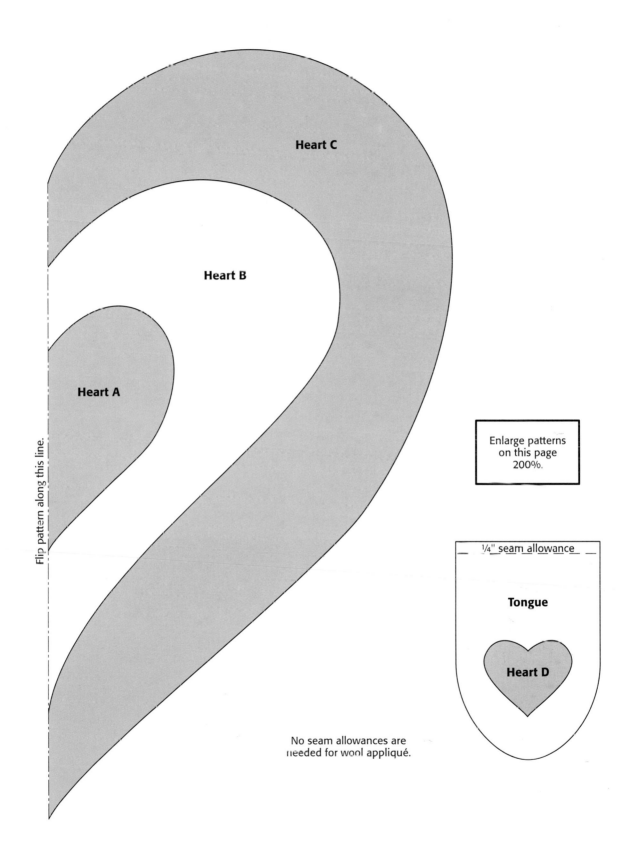

Heart C

Heart B

Heart A

Flip pattern along this line.

Enlarge patterns
on this page
200%.

¼" seam allowance

Tongue

Heart D

No seam allowances are
needed for wool appliqué.

HEARTS

"I've included two options for hooked rugs with hearts: a square Nine of Hearts rug done in shades of blue as well as an eight-heart rug hooked in assorted colors. The simple but pleasing hearts make a striking impression, whether you make one project or both."

—POLLY MINICK

Nine of Hearts Rug

Finished rug size: 23" x 23"

Materials

Wool yardage amounts are estimated, based on 60"-wide fabric. (See "How Much Wool Do You Need?" on page 125 for more information on estimating yardage before beginning any project.)

- ¼ yd. each of 3 shades of blue for hearts and the border
- 1 yd. of light blue for background
- 30" x 30" piece of backing fabric*
- 110" of binding tape for finishing

If you use a hoop, add 8" to the backing measurements. See "Rug Backing" on page 122 for more information on fabric measuring techniques and backing options.

Cutting

Cut your wool into size #8 or #9 strips, referring to "Cutting the Strips" on page 125. I recommend not cutting all the wool at once as it is prone to tangle into worms. However, if you're using several different light blues or medium blues for each heart, be sure to cut some strips from each fabric so that you can mix them up for better texture as you hook each heart.

Making the Rug

1. Transfer the design onto the backing of your choice, using the pattern (which needs to be enlarged 350%) on page 133. For details on transferring patterns, see the directions on page 123 in "Rug Hooking Basics."

2. Hook each heart in one shade of blue, starting along the outline edge and filling in. Note, however, that you can use more than one fabric for each shade of blue. For instance, you could combine a light blue, tweed, solid, and check in one heart to give it more visual texture. By starting along the outline edge, your loops will follow the form of the heart rather than lining up in straight vertical rows.

3. Hook the background using the light blue, beginning around the hearts.

4. Gather scraps from the hearts and use them to hook the border in a hit-or-miss random stripe pattern. (See "Borders" on page 128 for more details.)

Finishing

1. Finish your rug using binding tape. (For tips on tape application and other finishing options, see "Finishing Your Rug" on page 130.)

2. Steam and block the rug, referring to "Blocking" on page 130.

3. Sew on an identification tag, referring to "Signing Your Rug" on page 131 for various options.

HEARTS RUG

Finished rug size: 16" x 32"

Materials

Wool yardage amounts are estimated, based on 60"-wide fabric. (See "How Much Wool Do You Need?" on page 125 for more information on estimating yardage before beginning any project.)

- ♥ ¼ yd. each of 8 different colors for hearts and border
- ♥ 1¼ yds. of antique black for background
- ♥ 24" x 42" piece of backing fabric*
- ♥ 130" of binding tape for finishing

*If you use a hoop, add 8" to the backing measurements. See "Rug Backing" on page 122 for more information on fabric measuring techniques and backing options.

Cutting

Cut your wool into size #8 or #9 strips, referring to "Cutting the Strips" on page 125. I recommend not cutting all the wool at once as it is prone to tangle into worms.

Making the Rug

1. Transfer the design onto your backing fabric, using the pattern, opposite, which needs to be enlarged 500%. For details on transferring patterns, see the directions on page 123 in "Rug Hooking Basics."

2. Hook each heart in a different color, starting along the outline edge and filling in. That way your loops will follow the form of the heart rather than lining up in straight vertical rows.

3. Hook the background in antique black, beginning around the hearts.

4. Gather scraps from the hearts and use them to hook the border in a hit-or-miss random stripe pattern. Simply hook straight lines with one strip and change colors when you need to add a new strip. (See "Borders" on page 128 for more details.)

Finishing

1. Finish your rug using binding tape. (For tips on tape application and other finishing options, see "Finishing Your Rug" on page 130.)

2. Steam and block the rug, referring to "Blocking" on page 130.

3. Sew on an identification tag, referring to "Signing Your Rug" on page 131 for various options.

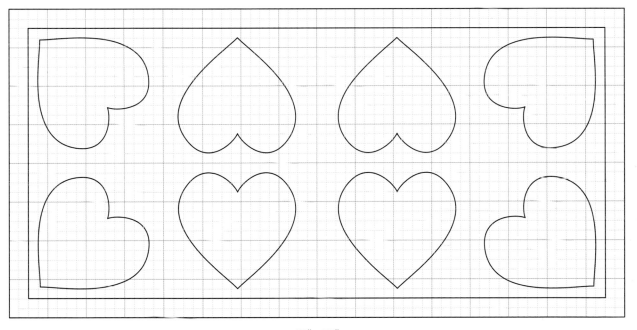

16" x 32"
1 square = ½"
Enlarge this pattern 500%.

OLD WEST SIDE

"This quilt was inspired by the charm of the nearly identical houses of the Old West Side neighborhood of Ann Arbor, Michigan, a historical district built by German settlers in the late nineteenth and early twentieth centuries. I lived there in the late 1980s and early 1990s, just around the corner from Murray Avenue and Mulholland. When I met my husband in 1994, I discovered he had been raised on Murray Avenue and that he had later bought another house on the same street. I made the original Old West Side quilt in 1990."

—LAURIE SIMPSON

"The Old West Side quilt was one of Laurie's first original quilt designs. After she left her job in a stockbroker's office to follow her dream, I asked to be her first customer and get an Old West Side quilt for myself. I made the companion rug to display in the guest room along with her beautiful quilt."

—POLLY MINICK

OLD WEST SIDE II QUILT

Finished quilt size: 93½" x 93½"

Finished block size: 13" x 13" • Finished Flying Geese size: 2" x 4"

Materials

Yardages are based on 42"-wide fabric.

★ 4¾ yds. total of assorted red plaids and prints for house blocks, sashing, and star appliqués

★ 3¾ yds. of white print for backgrounds

★ 3½ yds. of dark blue print for border and binding

★ 1½ yds. total of assorted medium and dark blue plaids and prints for house blocks and sashing squares

★ 8½ yds. of backing fabric

★ 98" x 98" piece of batting

Cutting

All measurements include ¼"-wide seam allowances. Patterns for the roof and sky are on pages 36 and 37 and include seam allowances. The pattern for the appliqué stars is on page 37 and does not include seam allowances.

From the white print, cut:
  25 B pieces, 2" x 6"
  50 D pieces, 2" x 3½"
  25 G pieces, 1½" x 7½"
  25 M pieces, 2" x 5½"
  25 template I
  25 template K
  25 template K reversed
  272 squares, 3¼" x 3¼"; cut once
    diagonally to yield 544 triangles
  80 strips, 1¼" x 4½"

From the assorted blue fabrics, cut:
  26 A pieces, 1¾" x 6"
  26 C pieces, 1¾" x 7½"
  26 D pieces, 2" x 3½"
  13 E pieces, 1½" x 3½"
  13 F pieces, 1½" x 4½"
  24 L pieces, 1½" x 2"
  16 squares, 2¾" x 2¾"
  13 template H
  12 template J

From the assorted red fabrics, cut:
  24 A pieces, 1¾" x 6"
  24 C pieces, 1¾" x 7½"
  24 D pieces, 2" x 3½"
  12 E pieces, 1½" x 3½"
  12 F pieces, 1½" x 4½"
  26 L pieces, 1½" x 2"
  60 squares, 5⅛" x 5⅛"; cut twice diagonally
    to yield 240 triangles
  100 strips, 1½" x 13½", for block borders
  12 template H
  13 template J
  40 stars for appliqué

From the dark blue print, cut on the lengthwise grain:
  2 border strips, 6½" x 81½"
  2 border strips, 6½" x 93½"

From the remaining dark blue print, cut:
  10 binding strips, 2¼" x 42"

Making the House Blocks

You'll need 25 House blocks for this quilt: 13 blue houses with red roofs and 12 red houses with blue roofs. In the quilt shown, the same blue fabric or red fabric was used throughout a single block. In the following directions, the red or blue fabric is simply designated as "dark" fabric to distinguish it from the white print background.

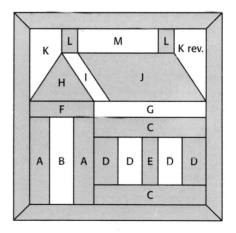

1. Sew a dark A piece to each long side of a white B piece. Press the seams toward the dark fabric.

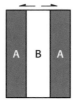

2. Sew the D and E pieces together as shown, so the dark and white fabrics alternate. Press the seams to one side.

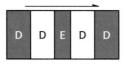

3. Sew the dark C pieces to the top and bottom of the D-E unit. Press the seams toward the C pieces.

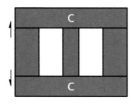

4. Sew the A-B unit to the left of the C-D-E unit. Press the seam toward A.

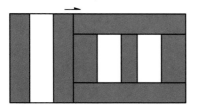

5. Sew a dark F piece to a white G piece. The F piece should be the same color as the house color used in the bottom row that you created in steps 1–4. Press toward the dark fabric. Sew this unit to the top of the bottom row. Press the seam toward the F-G row and set aside.

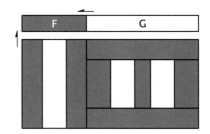

6. Sew a dark H, white I, and contrasting J together. Make sure H and J are not the same color, and that the H fabric matches the A-C-D-E-F ones. Press the seams toward the dark fabrics.

Sew a dark L (that matches the J piece) to either side of a white M piece. Press the seams to one side, and then attach the L-M unit to the top of the H-I-J unit, starting and stopping the seams ¼" from each end. Press the seam toward the H-I-J unit.

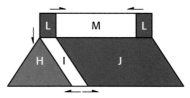

7. Sew the white K and reverse K pieces into place, pivoting at the seam intersections (indicated by dots in the illustration) to set in the angle. Press the seams to the outside.

Pivot seams at dots.

8. Sew the roof and house units together. Press.

9. To frame the block, center a 1½" x 13½" red strip on each side of the block. Sew the strips to the block, mitering the corners as described on page 116 in "Quiltmaking Basics." Press. Repeat to complete 25 House blocks.

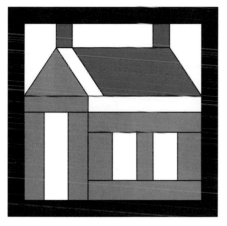

House Block
Make 25 total.

Making the Sashing

1. Sew a 3¼" white triangle to each short side of a red quarter-square triangle to make the Flying Geese units. Press seams to one side.

Flying Geese Unit
Make 240.

2. Sew the Flying Geese units together end to end in sets of six to make the sashing strips. Then sew a 1¼" x 4½" white strip to each end of the sashing strips. Press the seams in one direction. Make 40 of these units.

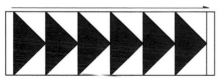

Sashing Strip
Make 40.

3. Sew a 3¼" white triangle to each side of a 2¾" blue square to make a cornerstone. Press the seams to the outside. Repeat to make a total of 16 units.

Cornerstone
Make 16.

Assembling the Quilt Top

1. Lay out the House blocks, Flying Geese sashing, and cornerstones into rows as shown in the quilt assembly diagram. The blue and red houses should alternate, starting with blue houses in the corners.

2. Sew the blocks and sashing together in rows. Press the seams toward the houses. Sew the sashing and cornerstones together into rows, and press the seams toward the cornerstones.

3. Sew the rows together. Press.

4. Place the two 6½" x 81½" dark blue border strips along the sides of the quilt top. Equally space nine stars on each side border. Adjust them as necessary so that they are visually centered, and pin or baste in place. Appliqué.

5. Sew the side borders to the quilt top. Press the seams toward the borders.

6. Place the two 6½" x 93½" dark blue border strips along the top and bottom of the quilt top. Arrange 11 stars on each border as you did for the side borders. Appliqué.

7. Sew the top and bottom borders to the quilt top. Press the seams toward the borders.

Finishing

1. Choose a quilting design and then follow the directions for marking the quilt top as described on page 116 in "Quiltmaking Basics."

2. From the backing fabric, cut two pieces, 42" x 100", and one piece 17" x 100". Remove the selvages and sew the pieces into a single piece measuring 100" x 100". Press the seams open.

3. Center and layer the quilt top and batting over the backing; baste the layers together.

4. Quilt as desired.

5. Trim the batting and backing even with the edges of the quilt top. Use the 2¼" x 42" dark blue strips to bind the quilt, referring to page 117 in "Quiltmaking Basics" as needed.

6. Make and attach a label to your quilt.

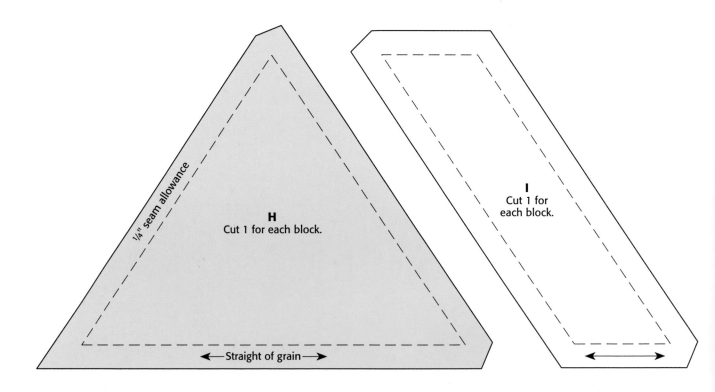

¼" seam allowance

H
Cut 1 for each block.

← Straight of grain →

I
Cut 1 for each block.

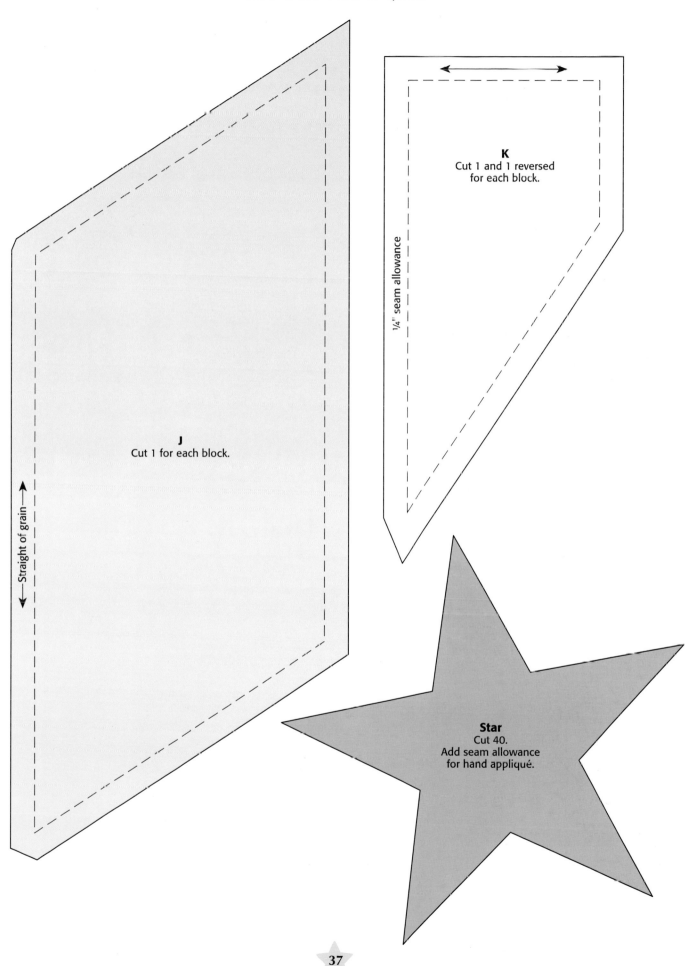

Straight of grain

J
Cut 1 for each block.

K
Cut 1 and 1 reversed
for each block.

¼" seam allowance

Star
Cut 40.
Add seam allowance
for hand appliqué.

OLD WEST SIDE RUG

Finished rug size: 34" x 47"

Materials

Wool yardage amounts are estimated, based on 60"-wide fabric. (See "How Much Wool Do You Need?" on page 125 for more information on estimating yardage before beginning any project.)

★ 1¼ yds. of soft pewter gray for background and windows

★ ¾ yd. of navy blue for border

★ ¾ yd. of old red for inner border and houses

★ ¼ yd. each of 4 different medium blues for houses and roofs

★ ¼ yd. each of 2 different reds for stars

★ ⅛ yd. each of 2 different darker blues and 4 different reds for houses and roofs

★ 42" x 60" piece of backing fabric*

★ 170" of binding tape for finishing

If you use a hoop, add 8" to the backing measurements. See "Rug Backing" on page 122 for more information on fabric measuring techniques and backing options.

Cutting

Cut your wool into size #8 or #9 strips, referring to "Cutting the Strips" on page 125. I recommend not cutting all the wool at once as it is prone to tangle into worms.

Making the Rug

1. Transfer the design onto your backing fabric, using the pattern (which needs to be enlarged 600%) on page 134. For details on transferring patterns, see the directions on page 123 in "Rug Hooking Basics."

2. Hook the houses, including the windows and doors.

3. Fill the background using the pewter gray. Begin by hooking the lines next to the houses and then filling in the larger areas.

4. Outline the border in red using one line of hooking.

5. Hook the stars in the border using the two ¼ yards of different reds. Fill in the border background with navy blue.

Finishing

1. Finish your rug using binding tape. (For tips on tape application and other finishing options, see "Finishing Your Rug" on page 130.)

2. Steam and block the rug, referring to "Blocking" on page 130.

3. Sew on an identification tag, referring to "Signing Your Rug" on page 131 for various options.

STARS ON STRIPES

"Laurie made this wonderful quilt for me. It's based on a quilt in the Museum of American Folk Art in Manhattan that was made in 1850 by an anonymous quiltmaker. The patriotic and historical theme is a natural for our home, where we proudly display many forms of the red, white, and blue."

—POLLY MINICK

"The inspiration for this pair of projects was an antique quilt as Polly mentioned. The original had the word 'Baby' stitched inside the center star. My interpretation has Polly's initials, and you can easily adapt that to your own name or initials."

—LAURIE SIMPSON

STARS ON STRIPES QUILT

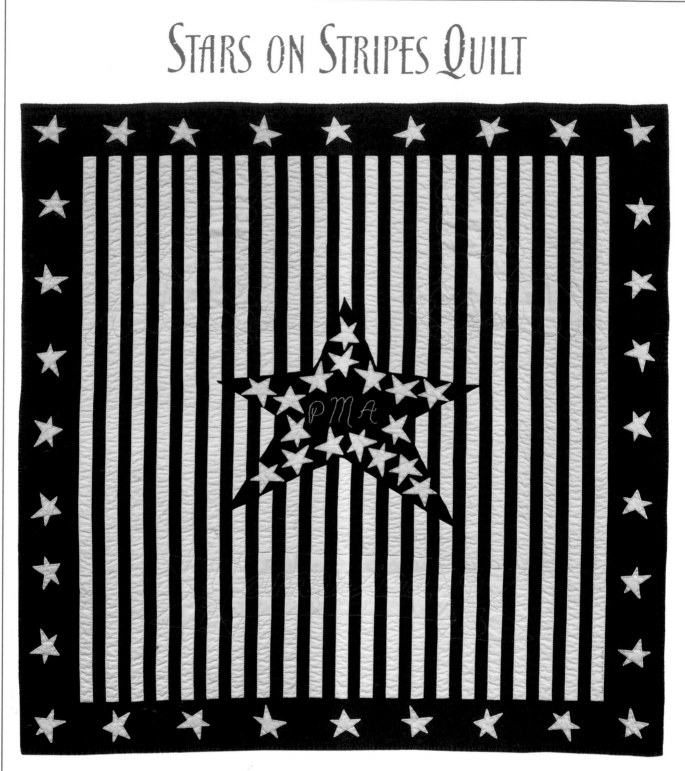

Finished quilt size: 49½" x 49½"

Materials

Wool yardage amounts are estimated, based on 60"-wide fabric. (See "How Much Wool Do You Need?" on page 125 for more information on estimating yardage before beginning any project.)

Note: While this is basically a red, white, and blue rug, use several shades of old red, off-white, and dark blue wool to make your rug more interesting.

★ 2 yds. total of assorted shades of dark blue

★ 2 yds. total of assorted shades of old red

★ 2 yds. total of assorted shades of off-white

★ 42" x 42" piece of backing fabric*

★ 170" of binding tape for finishing

*If you use a hoop, add 8" to the backing measurements. See "Rug Backing" on page 122 for more information on fabric measuring techniques and backing options.

Cutting

Cut your wool into size #8 or #9 strips, referring to "Cutting the Strips" on page 125. I recommend not cutting all the wool at once as it is prone to tangle into worms. However, be sure to cut some strips of each of the various red, white, and blue shades so that you can mix them up for better texture as you hook the stars and stripes.

Making the Rug

1. Transfer the design onto your backing fabric, using the pattern (which needs to be enlarged 600%) on page 135. For details on transferring patterns, see the directions on page 123 in "Rug Hooking Basics."

2. Hook the small off-white stars inside the large star at the center of the rug. Next, hook the large blue star using a mixture of dark blue wools.

3. Hook the stripes with a mixture of old red wools and off-white wools.

4. For the border, hook the small stars in off-white wool first. Then fill the area around the stars with an assortment of dark blue wools.

Finishing

1. Finish your rug using binding tape. (For tips on tape application and other finishing options, see "Finishing Your Rug" on page 130.)

2. Steam and block the rug, referring to "Blocking" on page 130.

3. Sew on an identification tag, referring to "Signing Your Rug" on page 131 for various options.

AIREDALES

"My husband and I share a love of Airedales, treasuring our own over the years and supporting Airedale Rescue. When Laurie wanted to pay homage to the popular Depression-era Scottie quilt with a twist, it seemed a natural for us to incorporate the Airedale into our projects. The particular inspiration for these projects is our precious family pet, Dixie."

—POLLY MINICK

Airedale Quilt

Finished quilt size: 73⅞" x 93⅜" • Finished block size: 12" x 12"

Materials

Yardages are based on 42"-wide fabric.

▲ 3 yds. of red fabric for border and binding

★ 2½ yds. total of assorted beige checks and plaids for background

★ 2 yds. of yellow plaid for setting triangles, sashing squares, and stars

★ ½ yd. total of assorted yellows for stars

★ 6 fat quarters (18" x 20") or assorted scraps of red prints for sashing and collars

★ 1½ yds. total (or at least 6 fat quarters) of assorted brown plaid scraps for Airedales

★ ⅜ yd. total of assorted black scraps for Airedales

★ 5½ yds. of backing fabric

★ 78" x 97" piece of batting

★ Template plastic

★ Black embroidery floss

Cutting

All measurements include ¼"-wide seam allowances. The star pattern is on page 54. The patterns for the dog, saddle, ear, and collar are on page 55. The appliqué patterns do not include seam allowances.

From the beige fabrics, cut:
18 squares, 13" x 13"

From the assorted red fat quarters, cut:
47 sashing strips, 2" x 12½"
18 dog collars

From the assorted brown plaids, cut:
18 dogs

From the black scraps, cut:
18 saddles
18 ears

From the yellow plaid, cut:
3 squares, 18¼" x 18¼"; cut twice diagonally to make 12 setting triangles (2 will be extra)
2 squares, 9⅜" x 9⅜"; cut once diagonally to make 4 corner triangles
17 squares, 2" x 2"
4 squares, 3⅜" x 3⅜"; cut twice diagonally to make 16 triangles (2 will be extra)
10 stars

From the assorted yellows, cut:
24 stars

From the red fabric, cut on the lengthwise grain:
2 border strips, 8½" x 78"
2 border strips, 8½" x 76"

From the remaining red fabric, cut:
9 binding strips, 2¼" x 42"

Making the Airedale Blocks

You'll need 18 appliqué Airedale blocks for this quilt. Use your favorite appliqué method, or refer to "Hand Appliqué" on page 113 and follow the appropriate instructions.

1. Cut a 13" x 13" square of transparent template plastic, and trace the Airedale design onto the plastic, placing the design on the diagonal.

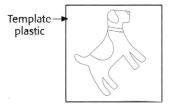

2. Align the appliqué pieces under the template. Appliqué them in the following order: dog, saddle, ear, collar.

3. Embroider the dog's nose using a satin stitch (see page 116 in "Quiltmaking Basics"). Press.

4. Trim the block to 12½" x 12½", making sure to trim on each side so that the Airedale is centered. Repeat to make a total of 18 Airedale blocks.

12½"

Make 18.

Assembling the Quilt Top

1. Lay out the blocks, red sashing strips, yellow plaid sashing squares and triangles, and setting triangles in diagonal rows. Sew the block and sashing-strip rows together as shown below, pressing seams toward the red sashing. Sew the sashing strips and sashing squares and triangles together, again pressing seams toward the red sashing. Sew the rows together and press the quilt top.

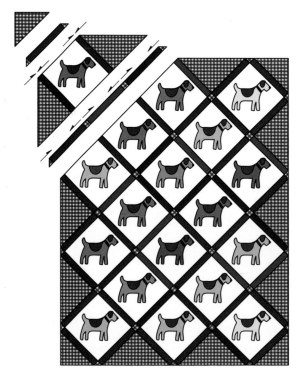

2. Lay the 8½" x 78" red strips along the sides of the quilt top. Evenly space nine stars on each strip. To help you position them, start by placing a star at the top, middle, and bottom of each strip. Next, place a star evenly between these stars. Finally, place the remaining four stars on each side border in the spaces between these stars.

3. Appliqué the stars into place and press the border.

4. Measure the quilt top from top to bottom to determine its length. Trim the side borders to this measurement, trimming equal amounts off each end to keep the stars centered. Attach the side borders and press the seams toward the borders.

5. On each of the 8½" x 76" red strips, place eight stars. To evenly space them, place the border strips along the top and bottom edges of the quilt top. Mark the quilt's center with chalk or a pin. Place four stars on each half of each border. Leave a little more space between the ends of the borders and the first and last stars than you have between each star.

6. Appliqué the stars into place and press the border.

7. Measure the quilt top across the center to determine its width. Trim the top and bottom borders to this measurement, trimming equal amounts off each end. Attach the top and bottom borders to the quilt top. Press seams toward the borders.

Finishing

1. Choose a quilting design and then follow the directions for marking the quilt top as described on page 116 in "Quiltmaking Basics."

2. From the backing fabric cut two pieces, 39½" x 97". Remove the selvages and join the pieces to make a 78" x 97" backing piece. Press the seam open.

3. Center and layer the quilt top and batting over the backing; baste the layers together.

4. Quilt as desired.

5. Trim the batting and backing even with the edges of the quilt top. Use the 2¼" x 42" red strips to bind the quilt, referring to page 117 in "Quiltmaking Basics" as needed.

6. Make and attach a label to your quilt.

Dixie makes herself at home on the Airedale quilt!

Star
Cut 34.

Add seam allowance for hand appliqué.

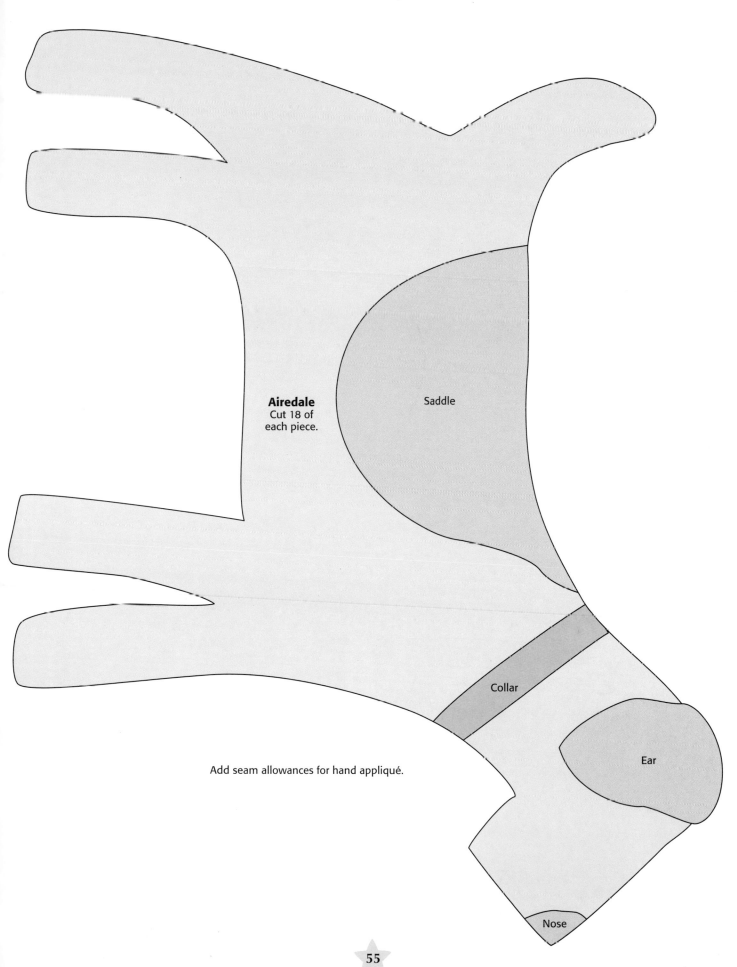

Airedale
Cut 18 of
each piece.

Saddle

Collar

Ear

Add seam allowances for hand appliqué.

Nose

Airedale Rug

Finished rug size: 33" x 22"

Two fine Airedales, Pepperoni and Dixie, looking cute as they pose on the front steps of Polly's house (above), while an antique fabric doll rests on the bed (left).

Materials

Wool yardage amounts are estimated, based on 60"-wide fabric. (See "How Much Wool Do You Need?" on page 125 for more information on estimating yardage before beginning any project.)

★ 1½ to 2 yds. total of assorted brick reds for background and stars

★ ¼ yd. of black for Airedale

★ ¼ yd. total of assorted tans for Airedale

★ ⅛ yd. of black-and-brown check for Airedale*

★ Scrap of contrasting red for collar

★ 1½ yds. total of 4 to 5 shades of mustard for scallops

★ Scraps of contrasting colors for outlining scallops

★ 30" x 42" piece of backing fabric**

★ 180" of binding tape for finishing

*You can substitute the black-and-brown check by overdyeing a more common black-and-white check with a brown dye. See "A Few Words about Dyeing" on page 122 for details.

**If you use a hoop, add 8" to the backing measurements. See "Rug Backing" on page 122 for more information on fabric measuring techniques and backing options.

Cutting

Cut your wool into size #8 or #9 strips, referring to "Cutting the Strips" on page 125. I recommend not cutting all the wool at once as it is prone to tangle into worms. However, be sure to cut some strips of each of the various reds, tans, and mustards so that you can mix them up for better texture as you hook the Airedale, stars, and background.

Making the Rug

1. Transfer the design onto your backing fabric, using the pattern (which needs to be enlarged 350%) on page 136. For details on transferring patterns, see the directions on page 123 in "Rug Hooking Basics."

2. Hook the Airedale using the black wool for the dog's "saddle" first, then the black-and-brown check for the area below the saddle. Finish the Airedale by hooking the tan wool. Hook the collar with the contrasting red.

3. Hook the stars in red, beginning with the outline edge and then filling in.

4. Outline the scallops in tans or golds. (See page 127 in "Rug Hooking Basics" to learn more about outlining.)

5. Hook the scallop backgrounds and the two points bordering the rug using the various mustard shades.

6. Fill the rug background in a brick red. If possible, use a variety of wool fabrics dyed in the same red formula to give rich texture to the background.

Finishing

1. Finish your rug using binding tape. (For tips on tape application and other finishing options, see "Finishing Your Rug" on page 130.)

2. Steam and block the rug, referring to "Blocking" on page 130.

3. Sew on an identification tag, referring to "Signing Your Rug" on page 131 for various options.

STAR-SPANGLED BANNER

"This quilt marches along with Polly's patriotic rug that she made to honor her son who was accepted into the U.S. Marine Officers Candidate School. Notice how the undulating quilted feathers make it look like the stripes are waving in a breeze. Notice, too, the odd number of stripes—this quilt has 15 rather than 13. That's just how our nation's flag looked back in 1795, after two new states had been added to the union.

The flag remained this way, with 15 stars and 15 stripes, until the War of 1812, and was the inspiration for Francis Scott Key's poem that eventually became the Star-Spangled Banner. Unlike the quilt, Polly's rug has 25 stars and just 10 stripes. Perfectly acceptable in a folk-art interpretation!"

—LAURIE SIMPSON

STAR-SPANGLED BANNER QUILT

Finished quilt size: 50" x 34¼"

Materials

Yardages are based on 42"-wide fabric.

★ 1½ yds. of red solid for stripes and binding

★ 1½ yds. of white solid for stripes and stars

★ ¾ yd. of navy print for star background and binding

★ 1¾ yds. of backing fabric

★ 38" x 54" piece of batting

Cutting

All measurements include ¼"-wide seam allowances. The star appliqué pattern is on page 63; it does not include seam allowances.

From the red solid, cut on the lengthwise grain:
4 strips, 2¾" x 27½"
4 strips, 2¾" x 48"
3 binding strips, 2¼" x length of fabric

From the white solid, cut on the lengthwise grain:
4 strips, 2¾" x 27½"
3 strips, 2¾" x 48"
15 stars

From the navy print, cut:
1 rectangle, 19½" x 22"
1 binding strip, 2¼" x 42"

This large wooden flag was made by Art and Hannah Stearns as a housewarming gift for the Minicks.

Making the Flag

1. Sew the 27½" red and white strips together, alternating the colors. Press seams toward the red stripes. Sew the 48" strips together in the same manner. Press seams toward the red stripes.

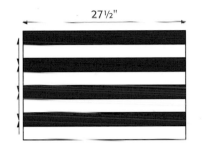

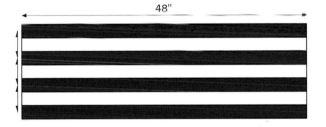

2. Using a washable chalk pencil or wheel, draw an 18¾" x 21" grid on the 19½" x 22" blue rectangle as shown in step 3 on page 62. The horizontal lines are 3⅝" apart, while the vertical lines are 3⅜" apart. Mark a dot in alternating blocks to indicate where to appliqué the stars.

3. Prepare 15 white stars for appliqué. Center a star in each grid square marked with a dot and appliqué in place using your favorite appliqué method, or refer to "Hand Appliqué" on page 113 and follow the appropriate instructions. Trim the blue rectangle to 18½" x 21".

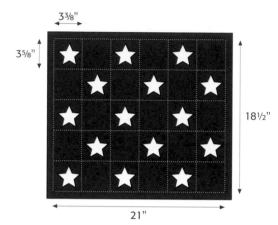

4. Sew one short edge of the canton (the navy field of stars) to the left short edge of the 27½"-long strip set, making sure that a red stripe is on top. Press the seam toward the blue fabric. Attach the long strip set to the bottom of the stars unit. Press the seam toward the long red stripe.

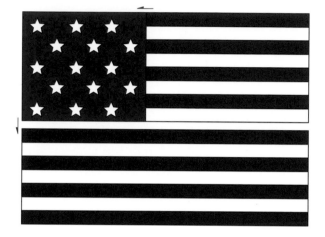

Finishing

1. Choose a quilting design and then follow the directions for marking the quilt top as described on page 116 in "Quiltmaking Basics."

2. Remove the selvages from the quilt backing. Center and layer the quilt top and batting over the backing; baste the layers together.

3. Quilt as desired.

4. Trim the batting and backing even with the edges of the quilt top.

5. Sew the three lengths of red binding together and then press in half lengthwise.

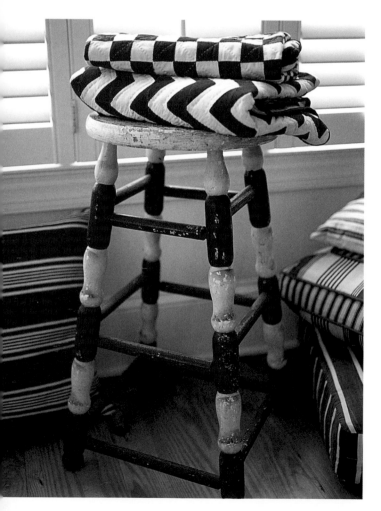

A pair of antique red-and-white crib quilts (tops acquired by Polly and quilted by Laurie) are perched on another vintage find, a charming painted stool.

6. Sew the red binding onto the quilt, starting on the top edge about 2" away from the blue fabric and leaving a tail about 3" long. Continue down the right side, along the bottom, and up the left side of the quilt, stopping approximately 3" from the blue fabric.

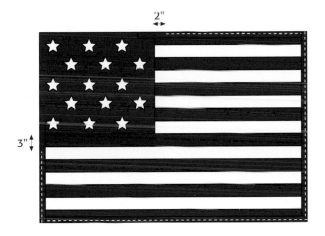

7. Unfold one end of the red binding and sew the blue binding to it, using a perpendicular rather than diagonal seam. Press the seam open, and then refold the binding. Continue sewing the binding around the quilt until it meets the red binding at the blue/red seam line. Join the ends as before and finish sewing the binding to the quilt.

8. Hand sew the binding to the back of the quilt. Make and attach a label to your quilt.

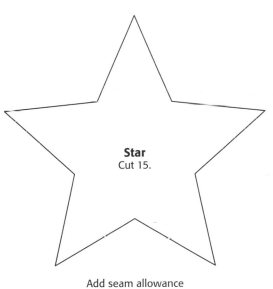

Star
Cut 15.

Add seam allowance
for hand appliqué.

Star-Spangled Banner Rug

Finished rug size: 38" x 30"

Materials

Wool yardage amounts are estimated, based on 60"-wide fabric. (See "How Much Wool Do You Need?" on page 125 for more information on estimating yardage before beginning any project.)

★ 1½ yds. total of assorted reds

★ 1½ yds. total of assorted off-whites

★ ¾ yd. total of assorted navy blues

★ 37" x 46" piece of backing fabric*

★ 140" of binding tape for finishing

If you use a hoop, add 8" to the backing measurements. See "Rug Backing" on page 122 for more information on fabric measuring techniques and backing options.

Cutting

Cut your wool into size #8 or #9 strips, referring to "Cutting the Strips" on page 125. I recommend not cutting all the wool at once as it is prone to tangle into worms. However, be sure to cut some strips of each of the various reds, off-whites, and navy blues so that you can mix them up for better texture as you hook the flag.

Making the Rug

1. Transfer the design onto your backing fabric, using the pattern (which needs to be enlarged 400%) on page 137. For details on transferring patterns, see the directions on page 123 in "Rug Hooking Basics."

2. Outline the edges of each star with off-white wool, and then fill each star with the same color.

3. Hook the star background with navy blue, beginning around the edges of the stars.

4. Hook the stripes on the flag with alternating red and off-white wool, beginning with red at the top position.

Finishing

1. Finish your rug using binding tape. (For tips on tape application and other finishing options, see "Finishing Your Rug" on page 130.)

2. Steam and block the rug, referring to "Blocking" on page 130.

3. Sew on an identification tag, referring to "Signing Your Rug" on page 131 for various options.

NOAH'S ARK

"I meet each year with a group of energetic and talented rug hookers on St. Simons Island, Georgia, to further our skills. The theme for our 2001 gathering was Noah's ark. My design mirrors the many blue arks in my collection of toy arks. Laurie made her quilt based on the same arks, but with stars in the center rather than as a border as I did in the rug."

—POLLY MINICK

Noah's Ark Rug

Finished rug size: 56" x 40¾"

Materials

Wool yardage amounts are estimated, based on 60" wide fabric, (See "How Much Wool Do You Need?" on page 125 for more information on estimating yardage before beginning any project.)

★ 3½ yds. total of antique blacks for background

★ 2 yds. total of 4 to 5 shades of medium blue for arks, stars, and flags

★ 1½ yds. total of 4 to 5 shades of red for roofs, stars, flags, and outlines

★ ⅛ yd. of off-white for flags

★ ⅛ yd. of pale olive green for ark trim

★ Scrap of darker olive green for ark trim

★ Scrap of pale gold for flagpoles

★ 47" x 62" piece of backing fabric*

★ 200" of binding tape for finishing

*If you use a hoop, add 8" to the backing measurements. See "Rug Backing" on page 122 for more information on fabric measuring techniques and backing options.

Cutting

Cut your wool into size #8 or #9 strips, referring to "Cutting the Strips" on page 125. I recommend not cutting all the wool at once as it is prone to tangle into worms. However, be sure to cut some strips of each of the various blues and reds so that you can mix them up for better texture as you hook the arks and stars.

Making the Rug

1. Transfer the design onto your backing fabric, using the pattern (which needs to be enlarged 600%) on page 138. For details on transferring patterns, see the directions on page 123 in "Rug Hooking Basics."

An early white New England step-back cupboard is filled with blue-and-white spongeware (top). Close-up detail of two arks, the inspiration for these projects (bottom).

2. Hook the arks in medium blue wools, beginning with the largest ark. Hook the ark roofs in red wools, with black accents. Hook the two stars in red, and hook the flags in shades of medium blue, red, and off-white. Hook the flagpoles in gold.

3. Use red wool to hook the lines that divide the arks, as well as the lines around and between the blue squares in the checkerboard border.

4. Using the same mixture of blues used in the arks, fill in the checkerboard squares and hook the stars in the border.

5. Using the antique black wool, hook the background, beginning with the areas surrounding the arks. Next, outline the outer edge of each of the two red stars and then fill the areas surrounding them. Finally, fill the border area.

Finishing

1. Finish your rug using binding tape. (For tips on tape application and other finishing options, see "Finishing Your Rug" on page 130.)

2. Steam and block the rug, referring to "Blocking" on page 130.

3. Sew on an identification tag, referring to "Signing Your Rug" on page 131 for various options.

Noah's Ark Quilt

Finished quilt size: 60½" x 68½" • Finished block size: 8" x 8"

Materials

Yardages are based on 42"-wide fabric.

★ 3¼ yds. of black print for outer border and binding

★ 2 yds. total of assorted red prints for star backgrounds and ark roofs

★ 2 yds. total of assorted medium and dark blue prints for stars, arks, and inner border

★ ⅜ yd. of white print for doves and flags

★ ¼ yd. of khaki fabric for olive branches, windows, and flagpoles

★ 4⅜ yds. of backing fabric

★ 65" x 74" piece of batting

Cutting

All measurements include ¼"-wide seam allowances. The appliqué patterns are on pages 77–83; they do not include seam allowances.

From the assorted red prints, cut:
   20 squares, 9" x 9"
   Save the remaining red fabrics for appliqué.

From the assorted medium and dark blue prints, cut:
   20 stars
   80 squares, 1½" x 1½"
   Save the remaining blue fabrics for appliqué.

From the khaki fabric, cut:
   2 flagpoles
   10 olive leaves

From the white print fabric, cut:
   2 doves
   Save the remaining white print for flags.

From the black print, cut from the lengthwise grain:
   2 border strips, 13½" x 43½"
   2 border strips, 13½" x 61½"
   3 binding strips, 2¼" x 100"

From the remaining black print, cut:
   4 strips, 1½" x 42"; crosscut into 80 squares, 1½" x 1½"

Making the Star Blocks and Quilt Center

You'll need 20 appliqué star blocks for this quilt. Use the pattern on page 77 to make the star appliqués. Use your favorite appliqué method, or refer to "Hand Appliqué" on page 113 and follow the appropriate instructions.

1. Center a blue star in each 9" red square and appliqué. Trim each completed block to 8½" square.

8½"

Make 20.

2. Sew the blocks together into five rows of four blocks each. Press the seams in one direction for the first row, and in the opposite direction for the second row. Continue pressing the rows alternately in this manner.

3. Sew the five rows together and press the quilt top.

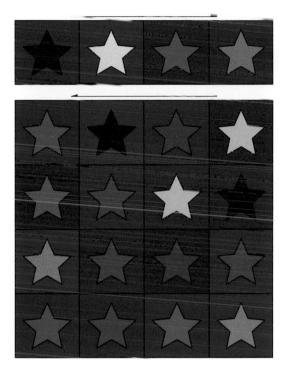

Making the Checkerboard Border

1. Make two strips of alternating black and blue squares. Each strip should have 32 squares, starting with a blue square and ending with a black square. Press the seams in one direction.

Make 2.

2. Sew these strips to the top and bottom of the star blocks. The top strip should start with a black square on the left, while the bottom strip should start with a blue square on the left. Press the seams toward the star blocks.

3. Make two more strips of alternating black and blue squares. Each strip should have 42 squares, starting with a blue square and ending with a black square. You will have some squares left over. Press the seams in one direction. Sew these strips to the sides of the star blocks so that the colors continue to alternate all the way around the quilt. Press the seams toward the star blocks.

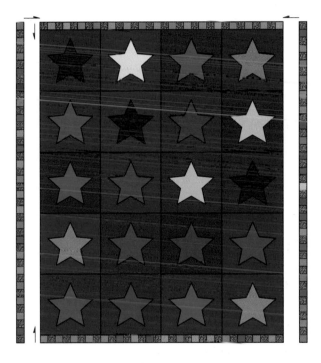

Appliquéing the Side Borders

Each appliqué border is different. Eight different ark patterns are used, and they are mixed and matched on the various side, top, and bottom borders. The following directions explain how to appliqué the various arks and their components. Refer to the quilt photograph on page 71 for placement.

1. For the left border, prepare the appliqué pieces for arks 1, 2, 3, and 4. Cut each roof from a different red print and each ark cabin from a different blue fabric. Note that the

body of ark 3 is strip pieced using strips in the following measurements: medium blue 1" x 9"; dark blue ¾" x 9"; medium blue 2" x 9"; dark blue 1" x 9". Sew the strips together, so that the ark can be appliquéd to the border as one unit.

2. Place a 13½" x 43½" black border strip along the left side of the quilt top. Arrange the four arks on the black strip, taking into account the seam allowances. Mark the ark placement with a chalk marker.

3. For each ark, appliqué the cabin first, followed by its roof. The windows are reverse appliquéd. To do this, cut ⅛" on the inside of the window markings, turn under the edges along the marked lines, and appliqué.

4. For ark 1, appliqué a ½" x 6" finished-width bias strip to the bottom of the keel. For ark 2, the keel is a ½" x 8" finished-width bias strip. For ark 3, add a ½" x 12½" finished-width bias strip keel to the bottom. For ark 4, add a ½" x 10" finished-width bias strip keel.

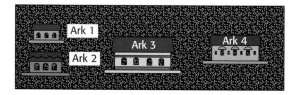

Left Border

5. For the right border, prepare the appliqué pieces for arks 5 and 6 and for another ark 3. Cut each roof from a different red print and each ark cabin from a different blue fabric. Note that the ark 5 cabin needs to be strip pieced first, as described in step 7.

6. Place a 13½" x 43½" black border strip along the right side of the quilt top. Arrange the three arks on the black strip, taking into account the seam allowances. Mark the ark placement with a chalk marker.

7. For ark 5, cut a 5" x 14" piece of dark blue fabric. Appliqué four light blue curved panels onto the dark blue fabric. Draw the window outlines onto the curved panels. Trim the completed rectangle to 4¾" x 13½", and attach a ¾" x 13½" medium blue strip to the top of this section and a 1" x 13½" strip to the bottom. Press the seams to the outside.

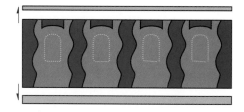

8. To make the flag, cut a 3" x 4¼" rectangle from the white print fabric. Appliqué the top red stripe into place, appliquéing only the bottom edge. Leave the top and side edges raw. Appliqué the center stripe and the last red stripe in place, sewing only the top and bottom edges, leaving the side edges raw. Appliqué the dark blue canton (star field) into place along the right and bottom edges. Leave the top and left edges of the canton raw. Press.

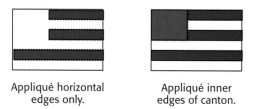

Appliqué horizontal edges only.   Appliqué inner edges of canton.

9. Appliqué the flag into place on the border, sewing along the top, right, and bottom edges. Leave the left side raw. Appliqué a khaki ½" x 5½" finished-width bias strip over the flag's raw edge to make the flagpole. Leave the bottom edge of the flagpole raw; it will be covered by the roof.

10. Use the scalloped roof pattern for this ark 5. (The alternate wavy roof is used on the bottom border.) Trace the entire roof shape onto red fabric. Include a ½" seam allowance all the way around the shape when you cut it out. Then, using two different shades of red fabrics, cut out the middle and top sections in the same manner.

    Appliqué the middle roof section onto this roof piece. Stitch only the bottom edge, leaving the sides and top edges raw. Appliqué the top section of the roof so that its bottom edge overlaps the top of the middle section. Stitch only along the bottom edge; leave the top and side edges raw. Trim any excess fabric from the roof back. Press.

11. Trim the edges of the roof so that you have a ¼" seam allowance around the entire roof. Appliqué the roof above ark 5. Reverse appliqué the windows in the ark. Finally, appliqué a single ½" x 17" finished-width bias strip into place along the bottom of the ark.

12. Appliqué ark 6, followed by the roof. Reverse appliqué the windows. Appliqué a single ½" x 5" finished-width bias strip in place at the bottom of the ark.

13. Referring to steps 1 and 4 above, strip piece the body of another ark 3. Appliqué the body and the roof to the border, reverse appliqué the windows, and appliqué a ½" x 12½" finished-width bias strip to the bottom of the ark. Press.

14. Measure the length of your quilt top and trim the two side borders to fit (approximately 42½" long). Sew the right and left borders to the sides of the quilt top. Press the seams toward the borders.

Right Border

Appliquéing the Top and Bottom Borders

1. Cut pieces for arks 2, 5, 7 (make two), and 8 using blues for the ark pieces and reds for the roofs. For this ark 5, use the roof with wavy lines. Also prepare two doves from the white print and two olive branches and 10 leaves from the khaki fabric.

2. Place a 13½" x 61½" black border strip along the bottom edge of the quilt top. Arrange an ark 7, an ark 5, and one dove on the black strip, taking into account seam allowances. Mark the positioning with a chalk marker.

3. For the ark 7 cabin, cut a dark blue strip 1¾" x 14¾" and a medium blue strip 4¼" x 14¾". Sew the strips together and press the seam allowance toward the dark blue fabric. Mark the window placement and cut away the fabric ⅛" inside these marks. Appliqué ark 7 in place, then appliqué the roof over it. Press. Appliqué a ½" x 19½" finished-width bias strip to the bottom of the ark.

Mark the windowpanes onto a dark blue fabric. Appliqué the windowpane fabric in place over the cutaway windows, then reverse appliqué the windowpanes.

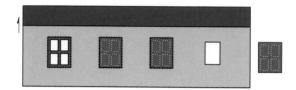

Appliqué windowpanes over cutout windows.

4. Prepare and appliqué ark 5 using the instructions in steps 7, 10, and 11 in "Appliquéing the Side Borders," except this time use the wavy roof instead of the scalloped roof. Note that this time ark 5 does not have a flag.

5. Appliqué a 10"-long, ½" finished-width khaki bias strip for the olive branch. Then appliqué the leaves and dove.

6. Measure the width of the quilt top and trim the border to this measurement (approximately 60½"). Sew the border to the bottom of the quilt top. Press the seam toward the border.

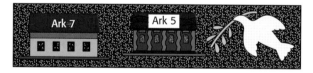

Bottom Border

7. Place the remaining 13½" x 61½" black border strip along the top of the quilt top. Arrange an ark 7, an ark 8, an ark 2, and a dove on the black strip, taking into account seam allowances. Mark the positioning with a chalk marker.

8. Make and appliqué the body of ark 7, as described in step 3 above.

9. Make and appliqué the flag for ark 7 by repeating the directions in steps 8 and 9 in "Appliquéing the Side Borders."

10. Appliqué the roof on top of ark 7 and the end of the flagpole. Appliqué a ½" x 19½" finished-width bias strip to the bottom of the ark.

11. Strip piece ark 8, using 7½"-long strips in the following widths, and then appliqué the ark to the border.

- ¾"-wide dark blue
- 1⅞"-wide medium blue
- 1"-wide dark blue

12. To prepare the roof for ark 8, cut a full roof with a ½" seam allowance from one shade of red. Then cut the top section of the roof from another shade of red and appliqué it on top of the full roof. Appliqué the bottom edge only, leaving the side and top edges raw. Trim any excess fabric from the roof back, leaving a ¼" seam allowance. Press.

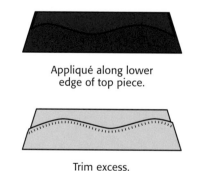

Appliqué along lower edge of top piece.

Trim excess.

13. Appliqué the roof, then reverse appliqué the windows. Appliqué a ½" x 10" finished-width bias strip to the bottom of the ark.

14. Appliqué the ark 2, followed by the roof. Reverse appliqué the windows. Appliqué a ½" x 8½" finished-width bias strip to the bottom of the ark.

15. Appliqué the olive branch, leaves, and dove as before.

16. Trim the border to the same length as your bottom border and sew it to the top of the quilt top. Press the seam toward the border.

Top Border

Finishing

1. Choose a quilting design and then follow the directions for marking the quilt top as described on page 116 in "Quiltmaking Basics."

2. From the backing fabric, cut two pieces, 33" x 74". Remove the selvages and sew them together to make a single 65" x 74" backing piece. Press the seam open.

3. Center and layer the quilt top and batting over the backing; baste the layers together.

4. Quilt as desired.

5. Trim the batting and backing even with the edges of the quilt top. Use the 2¼" x 100" black strips to bind the quilt, referring to page 117 of "Quiltmaking Basics" as needed.

6. Make and attach a label to your quilt.

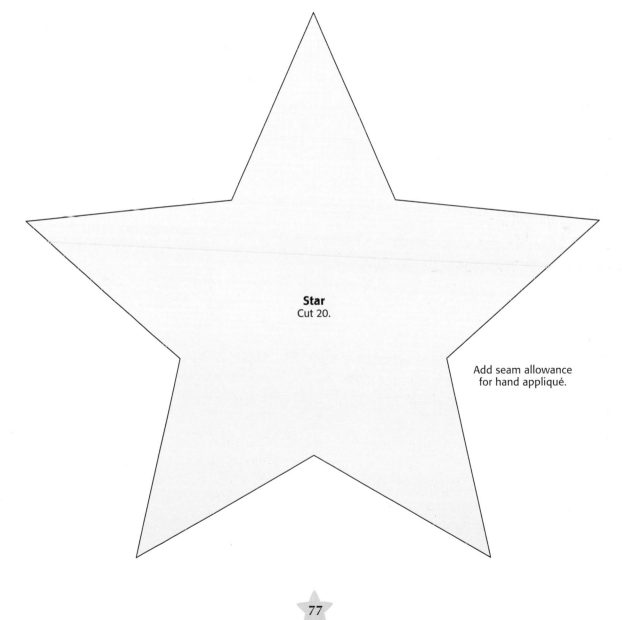

Star
Cut 20.

Add seam allowance
for hand appliqué.

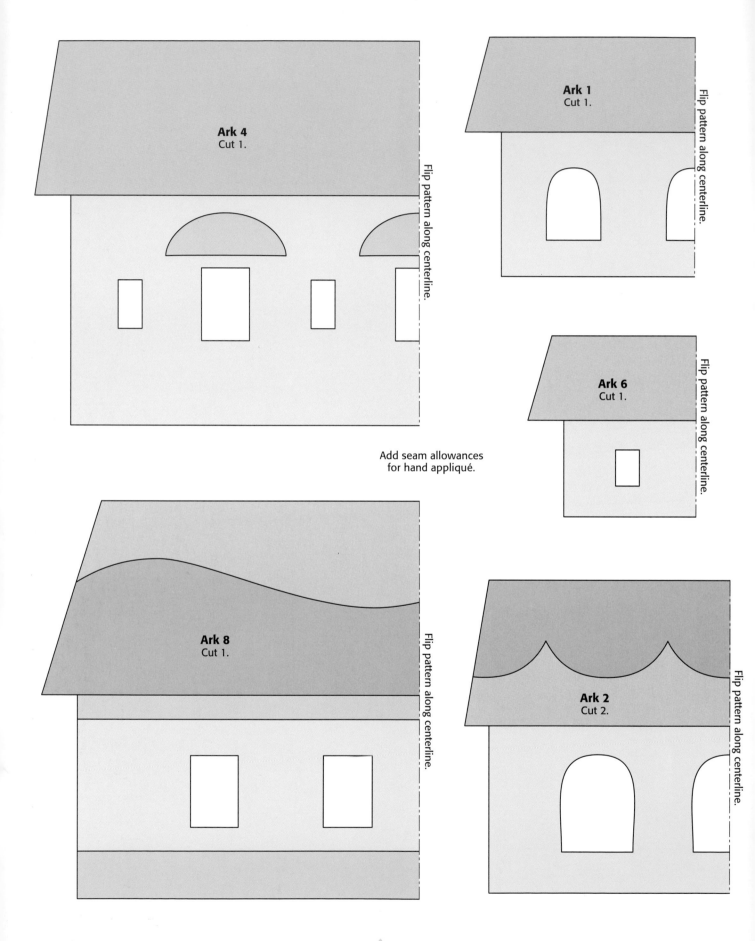

Ark 4
Cut 1.

Flip pattern along centerline.

Ark 1
Cut 1.

Flip pattern along centerline.

Add seam allowances
for hand appliqué.

Ark 6
Cut 1.

Flip pattern along centerline.

Ark 8
Cut 1.

Flip pattern along centerline.

Ark 2
Cut 2.

Flip pattern along centerline.

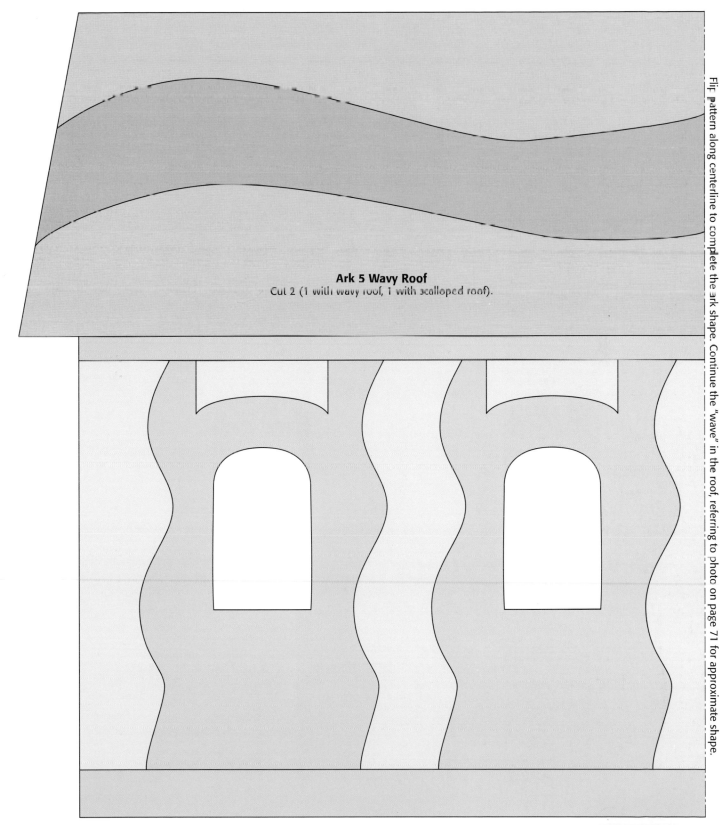

Ark 5 Wavy Roof
Cut 2 (1 with wavy roof, 1 with scalloped roof).

Flip pattern along centerline to complete the ark shape. Continue the "wave" in the roof, referring to photo on page 71 for approximate shape.

Add seam allowances
for hand appliqué.

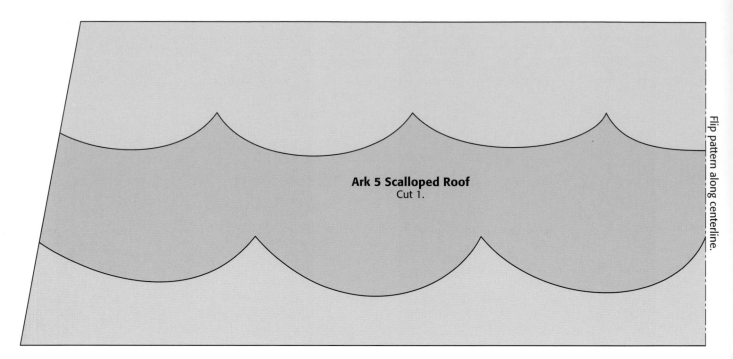

Ark 5 Scalloped Roof
Cut 1.

Flip pattern along centerline.

Add seam allowances
for hand appliqué.

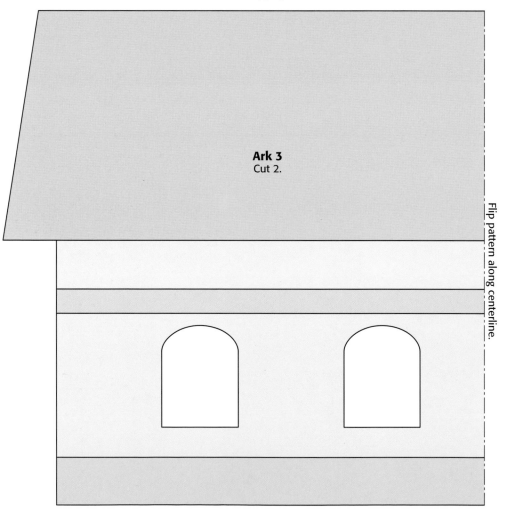

Ark 3
Cut 2.

Flip pattern along centerline.

Ark 7
Cut 2.

Flip pattern along centerline.

Add seam allowances
for hand appliqué.

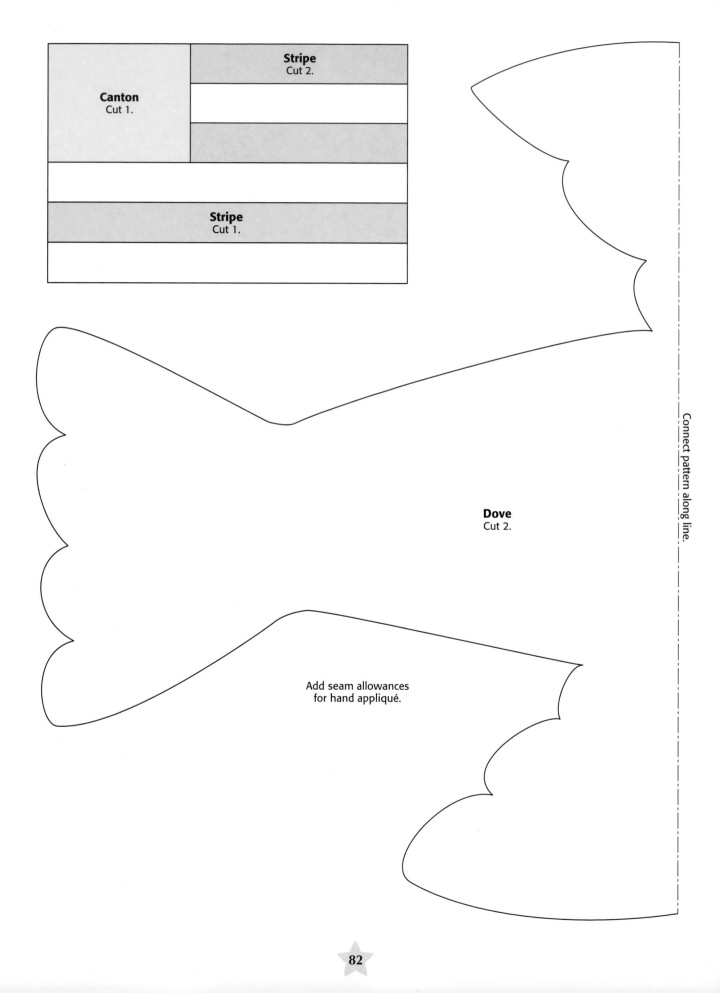

Stripe
Cut 2.

Canton
Cut 1.

Stripe
Cut 1.

Dove
Cut 2.

Add seam allowances
for hand appliqué.

Connect pattern along line.

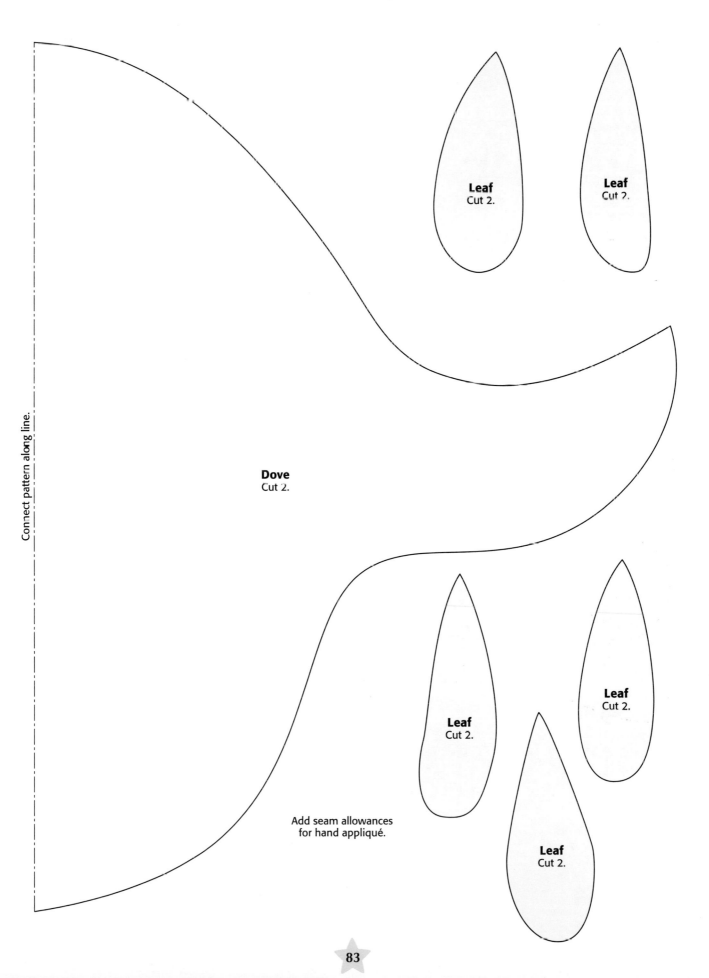

Connect pattern along line.

Leaf
Cut 2.

Leaf
Cut 2.

Dove
Cut 2.

Leaf
Cut 2.

Leaf
Cut 2.

Leaf
Cut 2.

Add seam allowances
for hand appliqué.

SAND PAILS

"Polly just loves vintage sand pails, and one of her most notable collections is of antique sand pails with patriotic themes. She authored a book with Karen Horman, Sand Pail Encyclopedia—A Complete Value Guide for Tin-Litho Toys. My light and breezy quilt works nicely with the rug she made to commemorate her favorite pails."

—LAURIE SIMPSON

Sand Pails Quilt

Finished quilt size: 38½" x 46½" • Finished block size: 11" x 15"

Materials

Yardages are based on 42"-wide fabric.

★ 2½ yds. total of assorted white and beige prints for background, appliqué, sashing, and binding

★ 1 yd. total of assorted red prints for appliqués and sashing

★ 1 yd. total of assorted blue prints for appliqués and sashing

★ Scrap of red-and-white striped fabric (¼"-wide stripes) for flag

★ Scrap of red-and-white striped fabric (1"-wide stripes) for shield

★ Red embroidery floss for flagpoles

★ 1½ yds. of backing fabric

★ 43" x 51" piece of batting

★ Washable fabric glue

Cutting

All measurements include ¼"-wide seam allowances. The appliqué patterns are on pages 91–93; they do not include seam allowances.

From the white and beige prints, cut:
  4 blocks, 12½" x 16½"
  4 border strips, 4½" x 34½"
  40 squares, 2⅞" x 2⅞"; cut once diagonally to make 80 triangles
  112 squares, 1⅞" x 1⅞"; cut once diagonally to make 224 triangles
  5 binding strips, 2¼" x 36"

From the red prints, cut:
  23 squares, 2⅞" x 2⅞"; cut once diagonally to make 46 triangles
  60 squares, 1⅞" x 1⅞"; cut once diagonally to make 120 triangles
  Save the remaining fabric for appliqué pails and handles.

From the blue prints, cut:
  23 squares, 2⅞" x 2⅞"; cut once diagonally to make 46 triangles
  60 squares, 1⅞" x 1⅞"; cut once diagonally to make 120 triangles
  Save the remaining fabric for appliqué pails and handles.

Making the Sand Pail Blocks

The sand pail patterns on pages 91–92 provide one-half of each design. For each pail, make a plastic template of the entire design, with stripe markings, stars, or other details. You can use this as an overlay to help you position the individual pieces as you appliqué each block.

1. Use a water-soluble marking pen or pencil and a light box or sunny window to trace the pails and handles on the center of the 12½" x 16½" blocks.

2. Make ⅛" finished-width bias strips, approximately 15" long, for each handle. Two of the baskets have red handles, two have blue handles. Using washable fabric glue, run a bead of glue along the marked handle line and glue the bias strips in place. You do not need to turn under the ends of the bias; they will be covered by the sand pail appliqués. Trim excess bias, leaving ½" beyond each end of the marked line.

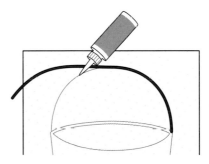

3. Appliqué the inside edge of the handle first, then appliqué the outside edge. Press.

4. For each sand pail cut a 9" x 11" rectangle—two from red fabric and two from dark blue fabric. Mark the perimeter of the sand pail onto each rectangle. You will appliqué the inside pail pieces and front decorations onto the pails first, and then trim the pails to size and appliqué them in place.

5. Appliqué dark blue inner pail pieces to the red pails, and medium blue inner pail pieces to the dark blue pails. (You can trim away the red or dark blue fabric from under the inside piece, but you may want to wait until all the decoration pieces have been added so the pail retains its stability.)

6. Add the decorations to each pail. Pail 1 is red with a single white star.

Pail 1

7. Pail 2 is red with a white band in the center and a dark blue band at the bottom. The blue band and the red band each have three small white appliqué stars. If desired, you can stitch the dark blue and red bands together by machine first, using a ¼" seam allowance. Then appliqué the white band to the pail.

Pail 2

8. Pail 3 is dark blue with a white band in the middle and a red band at the bottom. The word *SEA* is appliquéd on the white band. Make 20" of dark blue ⅛" finished-width bias for the letters. Use washable fabric glue to place the letters, and then appliqué them in place.

    For the flags, appliqué the blue canton (star field) onto a scrap of red-and-white striped fabric that is at least ¼" larger than the flag template. (You may want to select a blue-and-white star fabric for the canton.) Repeat for the second flag, reversing the placement of the canton. Press. Using two strands of red embroidery floss, embroider the flagpoles.

Pail 3

9. Pail 4 is dark blue with a white band appliquéd at the top. The white band has three small red stars and the bottom part of the pail has a shield emblem. For the shield, appliqué the dark blue top of the shield onto a larger piece of red-and-white striped fabric (1"-wide stripes). Appliqué only the side and top edges; leave the bottom edge raw. Press. Trim the striped fabric to the size of the shield template, adding a ⅛" seam allowance on the top and sides. Leave a ¼" seam allowance on the bottom edge. Sew the shield top and bottom together.

Pail 4

10. Using the full-size pail template, mark the outline of the pail again on the red rectangles and the blue rectangles if it has worn off during handling. Trim ⅛" away from the drawn line all the way around the pail. Appliqué each pail onto the block background, matching the pail color with the handle color. Press and trim the completed blocks to 11½" x 15½".

Making the Triangle-Square Strips

1. Sew each 1⅞" white and beige triangle to a 1⅞" red or blue triangle to make 224 small triangle squares. Press the seams toward the dark fabric. You'll have extra red and blue triangles, so make an assortment for a scrappier look.

2. Sew the small triangle squares together in 8 strips of 15 squares each for side sashing. The red and blue triangles should be in the upper right corners. Sew 8 more strips of 13 squares each, this time with the red and blue triangles in the lower right corners. These are for top and bottom block sashing. Press all seam allowances in the same direction.

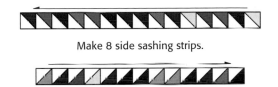

Make 8 side sashing strips.

Make 8 top and bottom sashing strips.

3. Sew each 2⅞" white and beige triangle to a 2⅞" red or blue triangle to make 80 triangle squares. Press the seams toward the dark fabric. You'll have a few extra red and blue triangles. Use a random amount of each fabric to give the quilt a scrappy look.

Make 80.

4. Sew 21 triangle squares together to make a 42½"-long side border. Make sure the red and blue triangles are in the upper right corners as shown in the illustration. Repeat to make a second border, then set aside.

Make 2 outer side borders.

5. In the same manner, make two borders of 19 squares each, measuring 38½" long. This time the red and blue triangles should be in the lower right corners. These will be the top and bottom borders. Set aside.

Make 1 top and 1 bottom outer border.

Assembling the Quilt Top

1. Sew strips with 15 small triangle squares to each side of the sand pail blocks. Press the seams toward the block. Then sew the strips with 13 small triangle squares to the top and bottom of the blocks. Press seam allowances toward the blocks.

2. Sew the blocks together in two rows of two blocks each, carefully matching the seam intersections. Press the seams open to distribute bulk.

3. Sew a white border strip to each side of the quilt. Press the seams toward the outside. Then sew a white border strip to the top and bottom of the quilt. Press seams toward the outside.

4. Sew the 42½"-long triangle-square strips to each side of the quilt top. Press seams toward the outside. Then sew the 38½"-long triangle-square strips to the top and bottom of the quilt top. Press seams toward the outside.

Finishing

1. Choose a quilting design and then follow the directions for marking the quilt top as described on page 116 in "Quiltmaking Basics."

2. Center and layer the quilt top and batting over the backing; baste the layers together.

3. Quilt as desired.

4. Trim the batting and backing even with the edges of the quilt top. Use the 2¼" x 36" white and beige strips to bind the quilt, referring to page 117 of "Quiltmaking Basics" as needed.

5. Make and attach a label to your quilt.

Pail 1

Pail 4

Flip patterns along centerline.

Add seam allowances
for hand appliqué.

Pail 3

Pail 2

Flip patterns along centerline.

Add seam allowances
for hand appliqué.

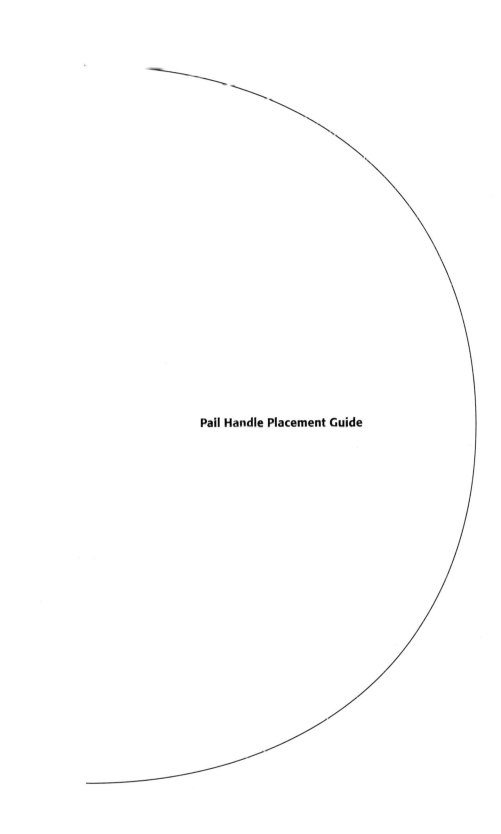

Pail Handle Placement Guide

Finished rug size: 65" x 24"

Materials

Wool yardage amounts are estimated, based on 60"-wide fabric. (See "How Much Wool Do You Need?" on page 125 for more information on estimating yardage before beginning any project.)

★ 3 yds. total of assorted medium blues for background

★ 1 yd. total of navy blues for pails and border

★ 1 yd. total of old reds for pails, narrow border, and lettering

★ ¾ yd. total of off-whites for pails

★ ⅛ yd. of pewter gray for pails

★ 32" x 73" piece of backing fabric*

★ 180" of binding tape for finishing

If you use a hoop, add 8" to the backing measurements. See "Rug Backing" on page 122 for more information on fabric measuring techniques and backing options.

Cutting

Cut your wool into size #8 or #9 strips, referring to "Cutting the Strips" on page 125. I recommend not cutting all the wool at once as it is prone to tangle into worms. However, be sure to cut some strips of each of the various colors, especially the assorted medium blues, so that you can mix them up for better texture as you hook the rug.

Making the Rug

1. Transfer the design onto your backing fabric, using the pattern (which needs to be enlarged 475%) on pages 140–41. For details on transferring patterns, see directions on page 123 in "Rug Hooking Basics."

2. Hook all the sand pails, referring to the rug photograph for color suggestions.

3. Hook the lettering that borders the rug in red wool. Next, hook one red line around the rug at the edge of the border.

4. Place a variety of medium blue strips in a basket. Randomly choose strips as you hook the background. Hook the areas inside the pail handles and outline the pails before filling the background.

5. Fill the border area outside the previously hooked red edge using navy blue wool.

Finishing

1. Finish your rug using binding tape. (For tips on tape application and other finishing options, see "Finishing Your Rug" on page 130.)

2. Steam and block the rug, referring to "Blocking" on page 130.

3. Sew on an identification tag, referring to "Finishing Your Rug" on page 131 for various options.

Part of Polly's extensive tin sand pail collection is displayed on a painted shelf (below), while more pails grace the edge of the master bathtub (left) and the fireplace mantel in the living room (right). Polly coauthored the *Sand Pail Encyclopedia* with friend Karen Horman in 2001.

MAKE IT YOURS

"I made this rug to encourage you to try your hand at designing your own rug. The process I used to create this rug is quite simple. You can easily draw your own motifs and use some of my techniques to design a rug of your own. The color scheme for my rug was somewhat dictated when I decided to use flags and shields in some of the squares. Of course, red, white, and blue is one of my favorite color schemes! When designing your rug, don't limit yourself to a few colors. Incorporate the ones you most enjoy."

—POLLY MINICK

MAKE IT YOURS RUG

Finished rug size: 56" x 32"

"For this particular rug I adapted shapes from other rugs in this book. I decided on a geometric style, using 8" square blocks. Some of the squares are filled with random stripes; others used templates. This style is a good option for first-time design. It lets you draw simple blocks or squares with a ruler and then fill in those areas as you choose. Notice how in the rug center I combined six squares to make an area large enough so I could fit large crossed flags, similar to those in the Sand Pails rug. I also reused the heart and large star motifs, this time having my grandkids write their names in the center so I could use their personal signatures. Other ways to incorporate special people into your rug is to trace their hands, use a child's artwork, or hook special dates into the rug. Think of your own creative ways to include elements about special people in your life in your next rug; there are many options."

—POLLY MINICK

Materials

Wool yardage amounts are estimated, based on 60"-wide fabric. (See "How Much Wool Do You Need?" on page 125 for more information on estimating yardage before beginning any project.)

★ 1½ yds. total of medium blues

★ 1½ yds. total of old reds

★ ½ yd. total of navy blues

★ ½ yd. total of light blues

★ ¼ yd. total of dark golds

★ ¼ yd. each of 6 to 8 different reds and blues (in addition to those listed above)

★ Scrap of lighter gold for flagpoles

★ 40" x 64" piece of backing fabric*

★ 200" of binding tape for finishing

If you use a hoop, add 8" to the backing measurements. See "Rug Backing" on page 122 for more information on fabric measuring techniques and backing options.

Cutting

Cut your wool into size #8 or #9 strips, referring to "Cutting the Strips" on page 125. I recommend not cutting all the wool at once as it is prone to tangle into worms. However, be sure to cut some strips of each of the various colors so that you can mix them up for better texture as you hook the rug.

Making the Rug

1. Transfer the design onto your backing fabric, using the pattern (which needs to be enlarged 600%) on page 139. For details on transferring patterns, see the directions on page 123 in "Rug Hooking Basics."

2. Hook the large block in the center of the rug, hooking the flags first and then the navy blue background.

3. Fill the squares surrounding the center block. I did the shields and flags before the hearts and stars. Hook the images, but leave the background to be filled later, as you may want to try different color choices after the images are in place.

4. Hook the hearts and stars. If you are using names, dates, or handwriting in the center as I did, hook these first, and then fill the hearts and stars, hooking around the writing. If you are hooking hearts and stars with no name or date, begin by outlining the hearts or stars and then fill them.

5. Hook the random stripes next. Doing these before the backgrounds in the other squares helped me choose the colors to go around the hearts and stars. If a color doesn't work, remove it and try another.

Finishing

1. Finish your rug using binding tape. (For tips on tape application and other finishing options, see "Finishing Your Rug" on page 130.)

2. Steam and block the rug, referring to "Blocking" on page 130.

3. Sew on an identification tag, referring to "Signing Your Rug" on page 131 for various options.

FOLK ART GALLERY

(Clockwise from left) Six-foot-tall Lady Liberty and Uncle Sam rugs welcome visitors. An 1870 child's wagon, painted for a parade, completes the scene. An early white doll bed is joined by a stack of contemporary pantry boxes. A patriotic birdhouse overlooks the marsh by Polly's home. Toy arks were the inspiration for the Noah's Ark rug and quilt. A collection of rolled-up rugs displayed in a charming two-handled painted basket nicely complements the Folk Art Stars projects.

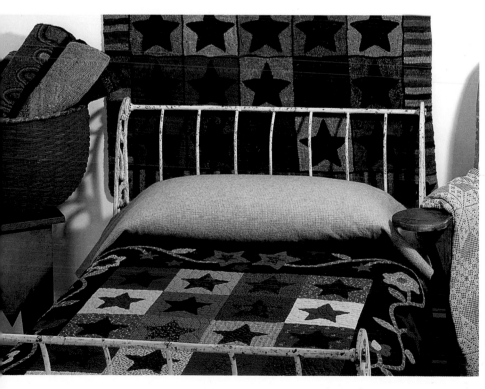

(Clockwise from right) Laurie stitched orphan antique quilt blocks of Polly's into small doll quilts, which are displayed on a grand-daughter's doll bed. Polly's iron sleigh bed is decked out with crisp white linens and Laurie's Sailboat quilt made of reproduction and antique fabrics. Cast-iron sailors and wooden sailboats add to the nautical theme, while antique red-and-white quilts stacked in a painted blue cupboard add softness to the room. Vintage drawers from a dry goods store and a white Shaker pantry box show off antique sewing tools and a collection of reproduction and antique indigo fabrics. Cast-iron sailor salutes you!

(Clockwise from left) Laurie's very first prize-winning quilt (made from a pattern by Laura Nownes published in *Star Quilts*, Quilt Digest Press) adds drama and flair to the dining room. Polly likes to take advantage of good weather on the back porch—a perfect place to hook. Laurie thinks that polka-dot horse rug will make a great quilt someday! Polly loves collecting red-white-and-blue items; here, an antique blue shelf holds bits of her collections. Folky Horses hangs over the sofa in the office; it's still one of Polly's favorites. A pair of folk art hens watch over the Three Chickens rug with very curious eyes.

(Clockwise from right) A vintage wine rack from a Maine hotel enjoys another life as a storage-and-display rack for dyed wools awaiting selection for Polly's next rug. What a visual treat! A hand-painted shop sign hangs above a large painted cupboard adorned with blue decorated stoneware crocks. Geometric with Hearts and Flags hangs in Polly's master bedroom. A wall of vintage game boards signals fun. Red-white-and-blue pencils stand behind a tiny salesman's sample of a red Windsor chair.

Quiltmaking Basics

"All of the quilts in this book were made by hand—hand pieced, hand appliquéd, and hand quilted—with the exception of the Airedale quilt, which was machine quilted. However, that doesn't mean you can't use machine techniques to achieve results that are just as rewarding. While I'm sharing my methods with you, feel free to use your favorite methods or refer to the information here for tips or a new way of doing things that can make the process more enjoyable."

— LAURIE SIMPSON

Fabric

Your quilt will only be as good as your fabric, so use the best quality quilt-weight (or shirt-weight) fabric from quilt shops or online quilt suppliers.

I also like to use vintage fabric whenever I can, because it lends an authentic air to my folk art quilts. Use only vintage fabrics in pristine condition. Unused scraps and yardage can often be found from antique dealers and online auctions. Don't use fabric from old clothing. Any fabric that has been laundered a lot will wear much faster than unused fabric in your quilt.

If you want to use vintage fabric, be aware that it requires careful handling. For instance, some old fabrics are not as colorfast as modern ones, so take care when laundering them. I prefer to wash fabric in the machine, on the gentle cycle, with very little agitation. You could also use the soak cycle. I use cool water and Orvus paste soap, and then dry it in the machine on the gentle/cool setting.

To prevent any unpleasant surprises, I recommend prewashing and preshrinking all fabric—old and new. Remember to press fabric before cutting it to ensure accurate measurements. All quilts in this book are based on 42"-wide fabric after washing.

MORE IS BETTER!

When I select fabrics for a quilt, rather than choose a single fabric of a particular color, I prefer to use a variety of fabrics in different shades of that color. In the project materials lists, you'll see that I often call for "assorted blues" or scraps that total a certain yardage. It's just more fun to sew with lots of different fabrics, and the result is a quilt that's much more interesting to look at. My philosophy is "Why choose one red when 20 will do?"

So I recommend following the materials lists as guides to the total yardage needed, but feel free to mix things up, to add scraps here and there, and to make your quilt your own unique creation.

Supplies

Sewing machine: If you machine piece, you'll need a sewing machine in good working order with a straight stitch. A walking or darning foot is necessary for machine quilting.

Rotary-cutting tools: You will need a rotary cutter, cutting mat, and clear acrylic rulers in several sizes. The most useful ruler sizes for the quilts you'll find in this book are 6" x 24", 12½" x 12½", and 1" x 12".

Thread: Good-quality thread is as important as good fabric. For machine or hand piecing, use an all-purpose cotton or cotton-covered polyester thread. For appliqué, a cotton silk-finish is the most versatile. Silk thread has the benefit of being nearly invisible once sewn, but it is more difficult to work with because it's so slippery. I have found that a fine (60-weight) 100% cotton thread made for machine embroidery works well. A long-staple 100% cotton thread is best for machine and hand quilting.

Needles: For hand piecing, I like size 11 Sharps. The thinner the needle, the more stitches you can put on it at once. You can use the same needle for hand appliqué, but use Betweens for hand quilting.

Pins and appliqué glue: Long, fine straight pins are a necessity for piecing. Use small sequin pins or appliqué glue with a fine-tip applicator for appliqué purposes.

Sandpaper board: This is a necessary tool for marking cloth for hand piecing and appliqué. Glue fine-grade sandpaper onto a hard work surface such as wood or acrylic. The sandpaper holds the fabric in place while you mark it.

Scissors: Use good-quality, sharp scissors for cutting fabric. An older pair can be used to cut freezer paper or plastic templates. Small scissors with a sharp tip are best for appliqué. Appliqué scissors (scissors with a wide flange) are helpful for cutting away layers of fabric from under appliqué pieces.

Template plastic: Use clear or frosted plastic (available at quilt shops) to make accurate, long-lasting templates.

Marking tools: I have a large collection of marking tools as different fabrics require different markers. The most useful are a #2 sharp graphite or mechanical pencil, silver or yellow marking pencils, and chalk pencils in several colors. Be sure to keep all marking tools sharp so that your appliqué or hand-piecing seam lines are fine and accurate. It's a good idea to test all marking tools on a fabric scrap before you begin your project to make certain the marks can be removed easily.

Batting: The desired look of the quilt and the ease of quilting are the most important factors to consider when choosing quilt batting. Machine quilters generally favor a flat, cotton batting. For hand quilting, polyester batting is easier to needle, but most quilters prefer cotton or cotton-blend batting for the look and drape of the quilt. For the quilts in this book, I used 100% organic cotton batting because it most closely replicates the look of an antique quilt after it's been washed.

INSTANT ANTIQUE

To achieve the look of an antique quilt, use the same materials and techniques our ancestors did. Use organic batting without scrim to get the look of a traditional quilt. After the quilt is washed, the batting will shrink about 5%. When the batting shrinks, a small pucker appears around each quilting stitch, which creates the look and feel of a well-loved antique quilt.

Additional supplies: Other useful supplies include tracing paper, freezer paper, needle threader, thimble, finger cots, tape measure, bias bars, and seam ripper. And, of course, you'll need an iron for pressing.

Rotary Cutting

Using a rotary cutter, a mat, and an acrylic ruler will allow you to cut your fabric pieces more accurately and much more quickly than using a pair of scissors. The following steps describe how to rotary cut a 2" square. For more specifics on rotary-cutting techniques, consult *Shortcuts: A Concise Guide to Rotary Cutting,* by Donna Lynn Thomas (Martingale & Company, 1999).

1. Fold the fabric with the selvages together and align the fabric horizontally on a line on the cutting mat. Using a 6" x 24" clear ruler and your rotary cutter, make a fresh cut perpendicular to the selvages to make a straight edge.

2. Move the ruler so 2" of fabric shows underneath it.

3. After the strip is cut, pivot the cutting mat so the strip is horizontal to you. Cut the strip into 2" pieces to make 2" x 2" squares.

Piecing

While I prefer hand piecing, I realize many people like to machine piece, so I've covered the basics of each technique in this section.

Hand Piecing

Hand piecing is the traditional method of piecing a quilt. It's not practiced by many current quiltmakers, as most prefer the speed of a sewing machine. However, hand piecing can be a surprisingly productive way to make a quilt. Like the tortoise and the hare, slow and steady can win the race. Instead of waiting for a time when you can be in your sewing room, you can hand piece nearly anywhere. Aided by a small portable sewing kit, you can stitch quilt blocks while visiting, waiting for appointments, or during travel.

1. Rotary cut fabric pieces with a ¼" seam allowance added, just as for machine piecing. Lay the cut fabric on the sandpaper board to keep the fabric from distorting and to reduce pressure on the marking tool. Use an acrylic ruler and a pencil or marker of your choice to mark a scant ¼" (to take the width of the marking line into account) seam allowance onto the wrong side of each piece.

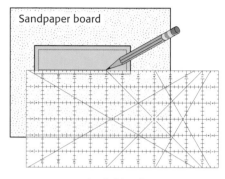

Mark stitching line.

2. The marked line is the sewing line. Use a sharp needle and cotton piecing thread to sew a small running stitch (about ¹⁄₁₆" long) on the line. Don't knot the thread at the end; take a small stitch (a backstitch) on top of your first stitch to secure it. Start and stop at the sewing lines. Don't sew into the seam allowances.

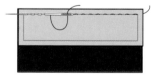

3. To end the sewing line, take a small stitch on top of your last stitch and pull your needle through the loop of the last stitch to make a knot. When you come to an intersection of seam lines, make an extra stitch to anchor your pieces. Check to be sure you're sewing on the line on both the front and back of your piecing. Also take a backstitch every time you fill a needle with stitches—about every 1½" to 2".

Machine Piecing

If you prefer to machine piece your quilt, you do not have to mark the stitching line on your patches. Each project gives cutting directions that include the ¼" seam allowances on all pieces. You simply need to maintain a consistent ¼"-wide seam allowance as you feed the patches through your machine. Otherwise, the blocks will not be the desired finished size, and the sashing or border pieces will not fit properly.

Some machines have a special presser foot that measures exactly ¼" from the center needle position to the edge of the foot. In this case, you can use the edge of the foot to guide your fabric. If your machine doesn't have such a foot, create a seam guide by placing the edge of a piece of tape or moleskin ¼" away from the needle.

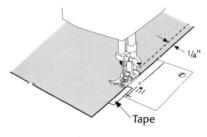

Tape

Pressing

For accurate piecing, whether by hand or machine, it's important to press seams to one side, usually toward the darker fabric. First press the seam flat to set the stitching, and then press the seam allowance in the desired direction. Press carefully. Don't push the iron back and forth as this can distort the fabric pieces.

Hand Appliqué

Needle-turn appliqué is my preferred appliqué method. Since so little preparation is required, I think it's the most time-efficient method of hand appliqué. Feel free to substitute an appliqué technique you prefer. *The Easy Art of Appliqué* by Mimi Dietrich and Roxi Eppler

(That Patchwork Place, 1994) is an excellent reference that covers hand, machine, and fusible appliqué techniques.

The following steps describe the basic technique for hand appliquéing. Please note that templates for appliqué do not include seam allowances.

1. Draw around the appliqué template to mark your sewing line. Cut ⅛" to ¼" away from this line. Pin or use appliqué glue to hold the piece in place.

2. Use a single thread and an appliqué needle (also known as a Sharp) to sew the piece into place. Starting on a straight edge or gentle curve, use the tip of the needle to turn under the seam allowance on the marked line. Turn under only about ½" ahead of where your needle comes up. Turn under just enough for no more than the next four or five stitches. Work from right to left if you are right-handed and hold the turned seam allowance between the thumb and forefinger of your left hand as you take small appliqué stitches. If you are left-handed, work from left to right and hold the work in your right hand. A seam allowance that will be covered by another piece does not need to be appliquéd down.

3. The appliqué stitch is worked from right to left (if you're right-handed). Begin by sewing up through the background fabric and into the crease of the seam allowance. Insert the needle into the background directly next to where it came into the appliqué piece. Let the needle travel about ⅛" to the left of the previous stitch and again come up into the crease of the folded edge (or a thread or two into the appliqué piece). Keep your stitches taut, but don't pull so tightly that the fabric puckers.

4. To end the stitching, pull the needle to the wrong side of the fabric. Take two small stitches into the background fabric behind

the appliqué piece. Don't let these stitches show on the front. Make knots by taking the needle through the loops of these stitches. Clip the thread, leaving a ½" tail.

LAYERED APPLIQUÉ

When appliquéing several layers for a quilt, appliqué the smallest piece onto the fabric beneath it, and then trim the underneath layer into the proper shape for appliqué, rather than cutting out each shape at the start. Continue appliquéing, trimming the last layer into the proper shape after all preceding fabrics are appliquéd onto it. Appliquéing pieces can pull fabric and shrink the piece underneath, but if you wait to cut the final layers after all preceding pieces are sewn, your appliqué will lie nice and smooth rather than becoming distorted.

When layering several pieces of appliqué on top of one another, press after adding each piece and reduce the bulk by cutting away the backing with appliqué scissors.

Appliquéing Outside Points

Begin taking smaller stitches closer together when you come toward an outside point. When you reach the point, take a stitch directly at the point, and then push the seam allowance under it and toward the side already sewn with the tip of your needle. Trim away some of the seam allowance, if necessary, for a perfect point. Continue to appliqué down as before.

Appliquéing Inside Points

Again, when approaching an inside point, start taking smaller, closer stitches about ½" before the point. Stitch past the point, return, and make another stitch at the point, stitching into the appliqué piece by a few more threads.

Glue Basting for Appliqué

Although you can pin or thread baste your appliqué shapes in place on the background, glue basting is an effective technique for needle-turn appliqué. It allows appliqué pieces to lie very flat against the background and has the benefit of no pins to catch your thread as you stitch. Use washable, water-based fabric glue, such as Roxanne's Glue-Baste-It, with a very fine applicator tip. You need only a few dots of glue to secure the fabric. The glue will wash out easily after your quilt is finished.

Bias Strips for Appliqué

An easy way to make bias stems is to use metal or nylon bias bars. You can find them at your local quilt shop or online. The following instructions are for making ⅛"-wide bias stems.

1. Use a rotary cutter, a mat, and an acrylic ruler to cut a piece of fabric on the bias ¾" wide.

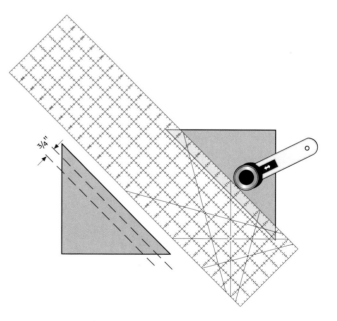

2. Fold the strip in half lengthwise with the wrong sides together. Sew ⅛" from the raw edge. Trim the seam allowance close to the stitching. Take care to stitch accurately so that you will be able to fit your bias bar into the tube you are making.

3. Insert the bias bar into the fabric tube, and twist the fabric to bring the seam to the center of the flat side of the bar. Using an iron on the steam setting, press the seam to one side. Press the other side. Slide the bar through the strip, pressing as you go, until the entire strip is pressed.

Reverse Appliqué

Reverse appliqué is just as easy as regular appliqué, so don't be intimidated. I find reverse appliqué is useful for stitching small shapes. It's often easier to use this technique, which involves cutting away part of the top fabric to let the underneath fabric show, rather than to appliqué a small shape on top. Here is how to reverse appliqué the windows for the Noah's Ark quilt.

1. Draw the window design on your already appliquéd house/ark fabric.

2. Cut slits to each corner of the reverse appliqué area, taking care not to cut into the background fabric.

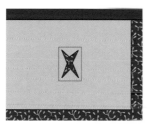

3. Cut away the excess fabric in the center of the window, leaving at least ⅛" on each edge for a seam allowance. With your needle, tuck each side of the window under until the fabric is pushed under the drawn line.

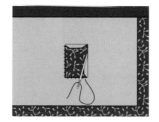

4. Appliqué on this line all the way around as you would for regular needle-turn appliqué.

Yo-Yos

You'll need to make yo-yos for the centers of the flowers in the Folk Art Stars quilt on page 10. Here's how to do it.

1. Cut a circle 2½" to 3" in diameter. (A juice glass works well as a template.) Turn under the edge of the circle by approximately ⅛". Sew by hand close to the folded edge with a long running stitch.

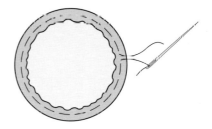

2. Continue sewing all the way around the circle. Keeping the sewing needle and thread attached, pull the thread taut to gather up the yo-yo.

3. Take several small stitches to secure the gathers, and knot the thread.

4. You can attach the yo-yos with an invisible appliqué stitch as used for needle-turn appliqué, or you can attach them with a blanket stitch (see page 116).

Embroidery Details

A couple of the quilts in this book have embroidery details. The specific stitches are shown here.

Outline Stitch

You'll use an outline stitch to embroider the inside of the center star in the Stars on Stripes quilt on page 42. To make the stitch, bring the needle up from behind the fabric and put the needle back down approximately ⅛" to the right. Bring the needle back through at the midpoint of the stitch you just made, coming up on the bottom side of the stitch.

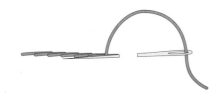

Blanket Stitch

This stitch is used to secure the wool pieces of the Heart penny rug on page 19.

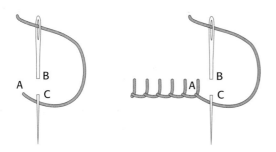

Satin Stitch

This stitch is used to fill in shapes, such as the noses in the Airedale quilt on page 50.

Mitered Corners

The house blocks for the Old West Side II quilt are finished with a mitered corner border, described in the following steps.

1. Center each border strip along the sides of the house block and sew the strips to the block, starting and stopping ¼" from the corners of the block; leave the ends free.

2. Fold one free end at a right angle on top of the free end of the adjacent border. Press.

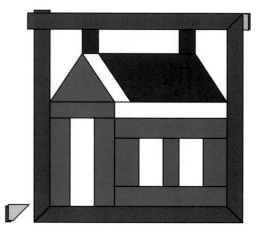

3. Appliqué or machine stitch the mitered edge seam into place over the border strip beneath it. Trim the excess seam allowance. Repeat for each corner.

Marking the Quilt Top

After you have decided on a quilt design, mark the design onto your quilt top with a marking tool that can be washed away after your quilt is finished. Refer to "Supplies" on page 111 for various marking tools, and make sure you test your tools on fabric scraps before using them.

In addition to marking pencils, masking tape is useful for marking straight lines and grids. Tape only small areas at a time and remove the tape after quilting each day to make sure no tape residue remains.

Layering and Basting the Quilt

After the top is marked, layer the top, batting, and backing into a quilt "sandwich." The quilt backing and batting must be at least 4" larger than the quilt top. If the backing is pieced, press the seams open for easier quilting.

1. Spread the backing, wrong side up, on a clean, flat surface. Secure the edges with masking tape. Keep the back smooth, but not stretched too tight.

2. Spread the batting over the backing, smoothing out any wrinkles. Lay the quilt top over the batting and smooth it. Make sure to keep the quilt-top edges square with the backing and batting.

3. Baste the sandwich with needle and thread, rustproof safety pins, or a basting spray (following manufacturer's instructions). When basting with thread or pins, do so in a large grid pattern spaced every 6" to 8".

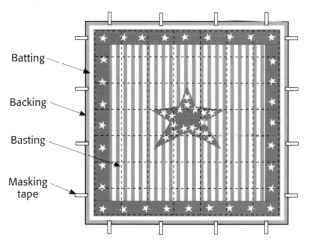

Batting

Backing

Basting

Masking tape

4. I also like to baste all around the edge of the quilt top, approximately ¼" from the edge, to keep the edges square and secure.

Hand Quilting

1. Thread a quilting needle with 18" of hand-quilting thread. Make a small knot at the end of the thread. Insert the needle in the top layer of the quilt about ½" from where you want to start quilting. Push the needle through the top and batting (but not the backing). Bring the needle up at the quilting line. Gently tug on the thread until the knot is buried into the quilt batting.

2. Make small, even running stitches through all the quilt layers on the quilting line.

3. To end your quilting thread, place the needle down near where the quilting thread comes out of the quilt. Wrap the thread around the needle three times. Put the needle back into the quilt top and batting (not the backing) one stitch length away. Bring the needle up approximately ½" and gently tug on the quilting thread until the knot you made is buried into the quilt batting. Clip the thread.

For more instructions on hand quilting, read *Loving Stitches: A Guide to Fine Hand Quilting* by Jeana Kimball (Martingale & Company).

Machine Quilting

Most of the quilts in this book are quilted by hand. If you prefer to quilt by machine, as was done for the Airedale quilt, by all means feel free to do so. Since I'm not a machine quilter, I'd recommend *Machine Quilting Made Easy* by Maurine Noble (Martingale & Company, 1994) as a handy guide on the subject.

Binding

Once you have finished quilting your project, trim the batting and backing even with the quilt top. To make a straight-grain binding, cut enough 2¼"-wide strips to go around all sides of your quilt plus an extra 6" to 8". Join the strips in one continuous length, using a diagonal seam to help distribute bulk. Pressing the seams open will also help to distribute bulk.

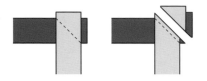

Joining Straight-Cut Strips

1. Fold the strip in half lengthwise with the wrong sides together. Press. Starting on a side of the quilt (not a corner), sew the binding on the quilt front using a ¼" seam allowance. Stop stitching ¼" from the corner of the quilt. Backstitch and cut the thread.

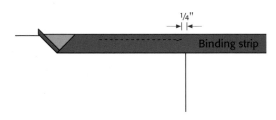

Binding strip

2. Turn the quilt so you can sew down the next side. Fold the binding up away from the quilt. Fold the binding back down upon itself. There will be a triangle of excess binding at the corner.

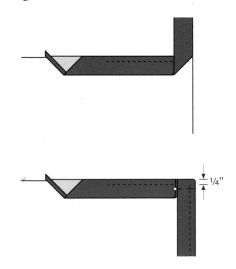

3. Begin to stitch again along the next side of the quilt using a ¼" seam allowance. Backstitch at the beginning to secure stitches, but stop stitching ¼" from both the top and right edges of the quilt.

4. Repeat the process for each corner. When you're within 3" to 4" of the beginning of the binding, tuck the starting edge into the end of the binding. Fold the end of the binding up ¼" so there is no raw edge. Trim if needed. Finish stitching the binding to the quilt.

5. Fold the binding over the raw edge of the quilt and sew the folded edge onto the quilt back using an appliqué stitch. A miter will form naturally at each corner as you fold the binding in place.

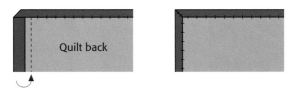

Quilt back

Labeling Your Quilt

It's important to label your quilt so the recipient and future generations will know the story behind it. You can cut a patch of fabric for a label or repeat a design from the front of the quilt, as I often like to do. Use a permanent fabric marker to sign your name, date, and any other pertinent information about your quilt on the label fabric. Appliqué the label onto the back of your quilt.

Rug Hooking Basics

"Any time you work on a rug, you are making a potential heirloom, so give your rug the attention to detail it deserves. I find that working with tools I love and quality materials makes the process enjoyable and the end result a rug to be cherished."

—POLLY MINICK

Supplies

High-quality materials are worth the investment. Most of the following can be purchased at fabric specialty stores and on the Internet. While I have my favorites, what works well for you might be different from what works best for me. So if possible, try out various hooks and frames before you commit. Remember to always use good lighting when rug hooking.

Hook. You'll find a variety of hook styles on the market. The handles vary from ball style to straight handle to very slim pencil styles, so you can choose the type that fits best in your hand. For the folk art or primitive-style rugs in this book, choose a hook with a sturdy shank for hooking wool up to ¼" wide. These are often referred to as "primitive hooks." Some models with finer shanks are available for use with narrower strips.

TRY BEFORE YOU BUY
Hooks come in different sizes and shapes. Test-drive them if possible before buying to decide which one works best for you and your designs. You may want to do the same with hoops and frames.

Machine cloth cutter or rotary cutter. You can cut wool strips using the same rotary cutter, mat, and acrylic ruler you use for quilting. There's even a specialty ruler-and-mat combination that has a grid with ¼" spacing for cutting strips quickly and easily with a rotary cutter.

Once you've become a dedicated rug hooker, you may want to invest in a cloth cutter to cut your wool strips easily and accurately. Fraser, Bliss, Rigby, and Townsend cutters all make cutting a breeze. See "Resources" on page 142 for company information.

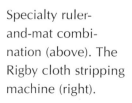

Specialty ruler-and-mat combination (above). The Rigby cloth stripping machine (right).

Wool. The preferred fabric for making hooked rugs is 100% wool. For lots more about wool, from where to find it to how to dye and cut it, see "Much Ado about Wool," below right.

Rug backing. You can use burlap, monk's cloth, or linen as the backing fabric for hooked rugs. For more on each of these fabrics, see "Rug Backing" on page 122.

Hoop or frame. You'll need to hold the backing fabric taut as you hook. You can do that by loading it either in a traditional quilting hoop or in a rug hooking frame. Frames come in both lap and floor models. Some have gripper teeth to hold the fabric taut and make loading and unloading easy. Personally, I started with a hoop and continue to use the same hoop today. It's all a matter of personal preference.

Rug binding. Just as with quilts, hooked rugs need to have their edges finished. It will prevent the backing fabric from fraying and give a nice, neat edge to your rug. You have a variety of choices when it comes to binding the edges of your rug. For more on these options, see "Finishing Your Rug" on page 130.

Scissors. You'll need basic fabric scissors for snipping off the ends of wool strips and for cutting your backing fabric to the correct size.

Custom or purchased pattern. In addition to the 10 hooked rug patterns in this book, you can find lots of other patterns available at quilt shops and specialty fabric stores. Or, you can choose to create your own unique pattern. You can trace patterns onto the backing fabric, or you can purchase patterns that have already been transferred for you.

Black permanent marker. You'll need one of these for transferring a printed pattern or your own designs onto your rug backing.

Optional Supplies

If (or I should say when!) you want to try your hand at dyeing wool, you'll need the following supplies:

Dyes and dye formulas. Cushing and ProChem make the most reliable dyes for wool. You'll also need a formula book (available at your local quilt shop, bookstore, or online retailer) that will specify exactly how much of each pigment to add to the mix to get the colors you want.

Dye equipment. You'll need a large pot, rubber gloves, wooden spoons, tongs, and vinegar for setting the color. Of course, the equipment you use for dyeing wool will be used exclusively for this purpose. What a good excuse to get out of cooking!

Color wheel. This handy device will help in planning your wool colors. Look for one at your local paint or art supply store.

For custom-designed rugs, you will need:

Red Dot tracer medium. This tracing material is available at most fabric stores. It's used to trace or draw patterns and then transfer them onto backing fabric.

Graph paper. You'll find this handy for sketching designs. It makes enlarging initial sketches easier because you can use the grid as a sizing guideline.

Much Ado about Wool

When I lecture on rug hooking, participants always have so many questions about wool, from where to find it and what type of wool to use to how to measure, cut, and store it. Since the foundation of rug hooking is fabric, and wool is the preferred choice, it's well worth spending time to learn more about this wonderful fiber. Fabrics other than wool have been used to hook rugs. You'll find that frugal rug hookers in the past used cotton, homespun, nylon, lace, and yarn. All the rugs in this book, however, are made from wool.

Where to Find Wool

If you're lucky enough to live near a quilt or fabric shop that carries wool for rug hooking, hurray! You can also buy new wool direct from woolen mills and via the Internet.

In addition to using new wool, you can recycle wool. I'm particularly fond of vintage wool. Finding it isn't always easy, so getting your hands on the perfect piece is quite a luxury. Some of the best places to find wool clothing are thrift shops, flea markets, garage sales—and even in your own attic. (Be careful about "shopping" at home, however. It's a great source of irritation to many to see their beloved shirts transformed into a rug!)

Be selective when buying wool clothing. Sometimes no matter how little you have to pay, it's just not a bargain. For instance, I don't recommend the gabardine wool often found in suits because it's flat, slick, and it ravels. Any loosely woven wool will make hooking difficult. On the other hand, skirts are a good option; they yield more fabric with fewer seams to undo. The backs of wool shirts also provide a nice-size chunk of wool you can use for hooking.

MEMORY WOOL

Consider using wool from the used clothing of beloved children, family, and friends. A friend told me about a happy memory of her grandmother asking to use her tattered baby blanket in a rug. My friend still has the remnants of her early blanket, lovingly hooked by her grandmother into a rug she treasures.

Determining Fiber Content

One question I'm often asked is how to tell if fabric is 100% wool or a blend. It's easy with new wool from your local fabric or quilt shop or woolen mills, as the fabric will be marked.

When shopping at rummage sales, flea markets, or thrift shops, look for the fiber content tags in the garments. The best choice is 100% wool, but a blend of 80% wool and 20% other fibers is acceptable. Anything less than the traditional 80–20 blend will cause you more grief than it is worth. So even if the color is perfect, my advice is to leave it on the rack.

Preparing and Storing Your Wool

Whether vintage or new, it's important to make sure your wool is clean and dry before using or storing it. The easiest way to do that is to wash the wool in your washing machine and dry it in your dryer. You'll be amazed just what a wonderful treatment it is for the wool. Wash your wool using a mild detergent and regular cold-water wash setting. Fabric softener is optional. Damp dry it in a dryer on medium heat to fluff the fibers, then lay it flat to air-dry and prevent felting. The process will clean the wool, give it body and texture, and keep it moth free.

When it comes to vintage wool, I recommend washing and drying the fabric twice. Wash the garment, then take apart the seams and rewash and dry all usable pieces.

After the wool is dry, it's ready to be used or stored. My suggestion is to store your wool in a room or closet set aside just for that purpose. Being able to see the wool and all its glorious colors and textures is so helpful when planning your next project. So even if your wool is kept in a closet, it's a good idea to keep it in clear plastic bins or on open shelves so you can see at a glance what you have. I've tried all ways of storing wool over the years, and I currently have mine in an antique wine bin. It's easy to access and I can instantly see what I have, which makes designing projects, hooking rugs, and keeping track of my inventory so much easier. When all the shades of blue are in one area, you won't have to go rooting for something you're sure must be hidden somewhere.

A Few Words about Dyeing

While the scope of this book can't cover the intricacies of dyeing wool, I do want to mention a little bit about overdyeing wool. You can certainly use wool "as-is"—just as you found it (except for washing it, of course). Some artists use only as-is wool and their work is beautiful. Personally, I prefer duller colors because they work well in my folk art–style rugs. I've always felt the need to tone down colors just a bit, and overdyeing wool is a way for me to achieve this.

Placing wool in a dye formula exactly the opposite of the original wool color is how the process works. For example, if you find bright red wool that's great quality, but the color is too bright for your rug, you can tone it down by dyeing it in a bath of green dye—the color that's opposite red on the color wheel. Use a weak solution of the green to overdye the red wool. If the color is still too bright, you can add more green dye until the desired shade of red is achieved.

A more radical way to overdye wool is to completely change the color. Light-colored wools such as off-white, cream, oatmeal, light gray, and tan can be altered quite easily to darker colors. Checks, plaids, tweeds, and other patterns that have light colors in them can often lend themselves nicely to overdyeing.

If you'd like to dye wool, your best bet is to use either Cushing or ProChem dyes, which are available at some quilt shops as well as online. Off-the-shelf commercial dyes are not recommended.

MARRYING COLORS

Marrying colors is a technique I used often before I had the nerve to jump into the world of dyeing. It's a simple way to blend different wool colors so that they're more coordinated, without using any dye.

Take several pieces of medium blue wool (or whatever color you're working with), put them in a pot of water, and bring the water to a boil. Once boiling, turn off the heat and let the pieces sit in the pot overnight to cool.

By boiling the water you will bring color out of the pieces you put in the pot. As the water cools, the color in the water seeps back into the wool at a more uniform rate. The pieces that started out as many different shades of medium blue now look a little more "matched" than before. The pieces will be different enough to give you nice texture when used together in a rug, but they'll at least look like they come from the same family.

Rug Backing

Today's rug hookers have three choices when it comes to rug-backing fabric: Scottish burlap, monk's cloth, and primitive linen. I've listed them in order from least to most expensive. All of them are suitable for rug backing, but like everything else, you may have a preference for one type over the other.

Most early rugs were hooked on burlap, and most often the burlap started life as a feed sack.

That is why so many rugs are somewhat the same size; rug hookers were limited to the size of the readily available backing material. I started out using burlap just as many rug hookers do. I quickly made the change to primitive linen, however, because I hook almost every day, and the feel of the linen is so much softer than the burlap.

Monk's cloth is a mid-price option, and it's also softer than burlap. So many of my friends use it that I decided to try it. I quickly realized that it was not for me, either, because it didn't stay taut enough in my hoop. The sagging cloth slowed down my hooking too much. However, if you use a frame that has a needle gripper system, you might love working with monk's cloth, just as most of my rug hooking friends do.

When preparing your backing fabric, make sure that it is at least 8" larger than your finished rug dimensions. If you'll be using a hoop for hooking, your fabric should be 16" larger. It's also a good idea to either tape around the edges with masking tape or serge the edges to prevent them from raveling as you work on your rug.

Getting Ready to Hook

Now that you know about all the equipment you'll need, you're almost ready to start hooking. But before we can actually hook loops of wool through the backing fabric, we need to transfer the pattern onto the backing fabric, select the wool for the project, and cut the wool into strips. You can purchase rug kits that contain the patterns already transferred to the backing fabric and all the wool you'll need already cut into strips. But to make the patterns in this book, and to branch out into your own designs, you'll need to know how to transfer designs and cut the wool yourself.

Transferring Patterns

If you are skilled enough to draw your design freehand onto the backing, go for it! If you don't feel comfortable doing this, you're in the same position I'm always in. We need to follow the steps below to transfer the pattern onto the backing fabric.

1. All of the rug patterns in this book need to be enlarged. We've presented the patterns as complete rug designs, drawn to scale but greatly reduced in size. You can use the grid behind the pattern as a guide for enlarging the pattern by hand, or you can take the pattern to your local copy shop and ask them to enlarge it by the percentage indicated on the pattern. Either way, you need to make a full-size pattern.

2. Once the design is the size you want for your rug, place the paper drawing down on a flat surface and lay a sheet of Red-Dot transfer paper over the design. Trace the design with a black permanent marker, being careful to trace over the entire design.

3. Lay the sheet of Red-Dot on top of the backing fabric, making sure the pattern is squared up with the grain lines of the fabric. (It will be easier for hooking straight lines of color in your pattern.) Tape the pattern in place and trace over it again with the black marker. For this step, go over the design using a somewhat heavy hand so the ink goes through the paper. When you lift the Red-Dot paper from the backing fabric you will see your design, but it may be quite faint. Trace over the design again with the marker so the outlines are very clear.

ENLARGING DESIGNS

If the design is not the actual size you want your rug to be, you can have the design enlarged to the exact size you want at a local copy store. Fortunately, I've found that most copy shops have staff willing to help with calculators. They can tell you the exact percentage you will need to enlarge the design to get the size you desire.

COOKIE CUTTER SHAPES

If you feel that drawing isn't your strong point, don't worry. The charm of primitive folk art rugs is in their simplicity. If you're still uncertain about drawing, try antique cookie cutters. After I found sets of nesting heart and star cookie cutters at an auction, I was soon on the lookout for other shapes. They're fabulous to use in rug design! I trace around the cutters and then enlarge or reduce the drawings at the local copy shop to use in my rug designs.

Keeping Track of Your Patterns

Once you trace over a design with black marker, the original outlines become a little blurred. Keeping a copy of the full-sized pattern will save you time in the future should you ever want to reuse the design.

I like to use plastic template sheets, available at quilt and fabric stores, to create full-sized templates of my designs. I store them by name in a file for easy reference. So when I need a heart or a star or an Airedale, I know just where to find them.

When you store your patterns, it's also good to note their source. It's fine to use the patterns in this book for your own use, of course, but do keep copyright in mind when you branch out into making your own rugs. It's great to get inspiration from other places, but remember when your grade-school teacher said not to copy the work of others? The same rule applies to rug design. Create your own designs; don't copy those of others. And if you're going to

show your rugs at shows or in a magazine, be sure to obtain the necessary copyrights to protect your original designs.

With the design transferred onto your backing, you are ready to start hooking your rug, unless you want to finish the edges first. There are a variety of ways you can bind your completed rug, and most of them can be done after hooking. However, you may want to read through the finishing techniques now and decide which method you'll use. That way, if you prefer, you can attach the binding first, before hooking. See "Finishing Your Rug" on page 130 for more information on the different options.

How Much Wool Do You Need?

The projects in this book specify how much wool you'll need of each color. But if you want to make any design changes, it's helpful to know how to estimate the amount of wool you need before you start cutting strips. Once you've cut the wool into strips, it's hard to estimate how much wool you have because the strips get tangled together.

To figure out approximately how much wool you need of a specific color, take the wool you have chosen for a certain image in the rug, and fold the wool to the size of the image. Opinions differ on determining wool requirements, but I always figure on four layers of wool, or four times the size of the area to be covered. If you don't have the wool yet and you need to purchase it, simply measure the area on the rug and multiply it by four. For instance, if you need to cover a 3" x 3" house, you'll need a 3" x 12" strip or a 6" x 6" square of wool.

Note that yardage requirements for the projects in this book are all based on four times the area to be covered. Depending on how closely together you pack your loops, you may need closer to five times the area. The yardages are based on the amount of wool I needed to complete the rugs.

Cutting the Strips

Most rug hookers use a strip cutter to cut their wool, but it is perfectly acceptable to cut strips by hand or with a rotary cutter and ruler if you don't have a strip cutter. The strip width is referred to by a numbering system used for the strip cutters, rather than by dimension. So even if you don't use a strip cutter, you'll need to know how the system works.

There are four major brands of strip cutters. Most of the models cut fabric into two or three strips at a time. They all use the same numbering system, although the actual strip width may vary a little bit from one brand to another. Basically, the number associated with the strip width represents increments in $\frac{1}{32}$ of an inch, as shown in the following chart.

Strip Size	Strip Width
#3	$\frac{3}{32}$"
#4	$\frac{4}{32}$" ($\frac{1}{8}$")
#5	$\frac{5}{32}$"
#6	$\frac{6}{32}$" ($\frac{3}{16}$")
#7	$\frac{7}{32}$"
#8	$\frac{8}{32}$" ($\frac{1}{4}$")
#9	$\frac{9}{32}$"

Most primitive rug hookers use a #6–#9 size cut, while traditional rug hookers use a size #3–#6 cut. Almost all machines on the market have cutters that range from a #2 cut up to a #9 or #10 cut. I always use a #8 or #9 cut. If you plan to rotary cut your strips, a #8 or ¼"-wide strip will be easy for you to measure and cut, so I recommend starting there.

To use a strip cutter, follow the directions provided by the manufacturer for your model. To cut strips with a rotary cutter, first make sure you're cutting along the grain of the fabric. Make a snip near one corner of the fabric and tear away the edge to give you a clean grain line to start your cutting. You may find it easier to cut strips wider than you need and then tear

DON'T CUT EVERYTHING AT ONCE

I never cut all the wool for a project at one time. First of all, storing fabric whole is much easier than figuring out what to do with cut strips, also known as worms. (Once you have a basket of strips tangled together, you'll see why they're called worms!) Secondly, measuring wool for projects is nearly impossible once it is cut into strips. Cut enough to get started and go back and cut as needed. And as you can see from the photograph of my studio on page 109, a cupboard of colorful wool, folded and stored awaiting your next project, can be beautiful.

them in half. You'll find it's easier to balance the long ruler on top of the wool that way, and this will give your rug an even more primitive look, as you'll have a frayed edge along one side of each strip. For instance, cut strips ½" instead of ¼" wide. Then make a small snip at the mid-point of one short end of the strip. Grip the two sides of the wool and tear the strip vertically.

Another way to cut strips with your rotary cutter is to purchase a special mat-and-ruler combination tool (shown on page 119) that is designed specifically for cutting rug hooking strips. The mat has a grid with lines spaced ¼" apart. You place the wool between the ruler and the mat, which are attached to each other so the ruler won't slip. Then you use your rotary cutter to slice the wool. See "Resources" on page 142 for information on these cutting systems as well as on strip cutters.

Basic Rug Hooking

By now I'm sure you're anxious to get hooking and pull your first loop. You've selected your equipment, transferred your design, cut your strips, and you're ready to get started. The good news is, in my opinion all the hard work is behind you. Now you can start the best part—hooking. Don't worry if at first it seems a little slow and tedious. Before long you will be comfortable with the technique and then you'll agree—this part is fun, rewarding, and relaxing.

How to Hook

I'm a right-handed hooker and the following directions are explained from my point of view. If you're left-handed, simply switch directions and hold the wool and hook in opposite hands from what I've indicated.

1. Put the backing fabric in your hoop or frame so that it is taut.

2. Take a strip of your wool, cut in the width you have decided is best for you. Hold the strip in your left hand under the backing material.

3. In your right hand, hold your hook as you would a pencil.

4. Poke the hook into the backing fabric and pull the wool strip through the backing so that the tail end pokes up through the fabric.

5. Repeat, this time pulling up a loop. Pull it up to your desired-length loop, about ⅜" long. You may want to experiment a little until you find the correct loop length for you. Soon it will become automatic to pull the loop exactly to your desired length.

6. Continue pulling loops through the backing fabric until you've come to the end of your wool strip. Then pull the tail up through the backing and snip the tail end to the length of your loops. (Keep a handheld vacuum or whisk broom close by for easy cleanup.)

7. When starting a new strip of wool, pull the tail up into the same hole in which the previous strip ended.

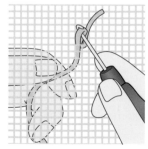
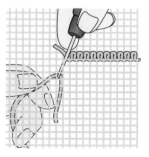

POLLY'S TIPS FOR SUCCESS

When you are beginning the process of hooking and pulling loops, you will want to concentrate on a few things and your rug will turn out great.

- Try to keep the height of the loops uniform, at least ⅜".

- Don't hook loops too tightly or they'll become disfigured. Skipping one or more holes in the weave of the backing fabric while hooking will help keep loops loose, yet fill in the surface quite nicely.

- Do not twist the wool strips. Use your hand below the backing material to keep the wool flat on the underside of the rug.

- Pull the tails up through the backing and snip the end from the top side to keep the underside neat and prevent raveling.

- For rug hookers, just as for children with crayons, staying inside the lines is important. Hooking inside the drawn lines keeps images at the proper size. Going outside—even a little—can throw off an entire design.

Getting Started

Now that you've practiced the motion of hooking, it's time to get started on your first project. I recommend starting to hook in the center of the rug where the primary design will be located. Hook all the designs in the rug, and then go back and fill in the background areas. Finally, hook the border.

Outlining

Outlining is a word you will hear and read often, especially if you are hooking rugs in the primitive style. Traditional rug hookers usually use more intricate shading and generally don't use this technique. To outline a shape such as an animal or flower, hook the perimeter of the shape first, then fill in the shape. The two parts of the design are often referred to as outline and fill.

BAG YOUR WOOL

This organizational technique works so well! When working with different wool colors for similar images such as Old West Side (page 38), Noah's Ark (page 68), and Sand Pails (page 94), set aside the amount of each color needed for each image. Place each color of wool in a plastic bag and number it. Write the corresponding number for the color on your rug backing for easy "hooking-by-number."

All about Color

Color is the most important aspect of any rug. I've said it before and believe it now more than ever, some 300 rugs later. Technique is important, but the color hits you before you have had a chance to look at the artist's technique. The designs are important, but they are purely a personal choice. You may prefer traditional, geometric, floral, or my love—folk art. But if the color doesn't appeal to you or the placement of it isn't right, the rug won't appeal to you either. Time will not improve poor color placement in a rug.

If you are working on a rug and putting in a color that is bothering you, stop and move on to another part of the rug. Go back to the offending color in a day or two. If it still bothers you—remove it. I was very hesitant to do this when I first started hooking rugs. I've gone back to a couple of rugs years later and pulled out the color that was bothering me, and I was sorry I waited so long to do it. It's easy to pull out the strips and replace them with another color—not at all like ripping out sewing mistakes!

COLOR VARIATIONS

Old colors (for example, the old red and off white mentioned in the Old West Side and Stars on Stripes rugs) are various wools (checks, plaids, stripes, and plain fabrics) dyed together in a single formula. After the dye process, the strips are cut and randomly mixed in a basket. When a rug uses a blend of these strips, the end result is eye-catching color depth and texture. The technique creates a more authentic antique look than that of the same wools dyed separately.

Develop Your Own Color Sense

I feel strongly that a person develops a signature in their rugs after a fashion. Whether you like to hook a certain image, have a flair for borders, or always use the same color palette, you're developing your own style. Color is certainly a signature for many people. Work in the colors you love, not just in the colors I've presented in the projects in this book. To determine your color palette, recognize the colors you like and use most often. Ask a friend for his or her opinion about your color choices. When you know your colors, appreciate them and use them freely.

My advice is to not plan a rug color around your wall paint or a favorite chair; we all know how often we like to redecorate. Plan the rug in colors you have always loved, and it will work for you always.

Don't be frightened by color. Do not let someone tell you that you "must" add a color to a rug that is not a color you like. Always try to be open to suggestions and learn as much as you can from someone willing to give time and attention to you and your rug. But remember, it is your rug and you have to live with it. If someone suggests that you add a color you despise, just say no! I have seen people put in a color they hate only to remove it as soon as they get home.

Borders

The choices for borders are truly endless, and again very personal. Not all rugs need to have a border, and yet some rugs are truly distinctive because of their wonderful borders. If you look through books and examine antique rugs, you'll see that many of them don't have borders while others have truly magnificent borders. When you're planning your project, try to visualize your rug design in its entirety when you begin, and make the decision then if you want a border or not. It's just like planning a quilt; some have borders and some are better off without them.

Ideas for Great Borders

While the projects in this book offer a variety of border options, at some point you'll like to plan borders of your own. Be creative and have fun with your borders. Take time to look through books of rugs. You will be introduced to a wonderful array of borders. Here are some simple ideas to keep in mind to help you create borders that are well suited to your rugs.

- Don't introduce an entirely new color in the border. It is best to pull colors from the center of the rug into the border. It doesn't have to be a predominant color, but one that was used in some fashion. Using a color for the first time in the border can make the border look as if it doesn't belong.

- Use an image from the center of your rug in the border. Use a star motif along the edges of a border, or some other simple shape that can be repeated.

- Use random stripes or a hit-or-miss border. For the hit-or-miss technique, gather scraps of the wools from your rug and use them randomly to fill in the border space. When you've finished hooking one strip, start with another color. The result is a happy mix of color and texture. These borders are fun and easy to do, and they allow you to use all the colors from the center of your rug. Hit-or-miss borders are often seen in antique rugs.

- Hook random stripes on the diagonal. This creates a nice look, but beware that it can also pull your backing out of whack just a bit. You can fix that by blocking the finished rug back into shape.

- For a rich, subtle look, use the background color of the center of the rug as the border color, too. Simply set the border apart from the rug center with one or two lines hooked in a contrasting color.

- Add more stripes. A border that I like to use frequently is the border you see on the Folk Art Stars rug on page 16 and opposite—stripes using all the colors in the rug. On this particular rug, I hooked three lines of one color before switching to the next color.

- Make corner squares. Another option for the corners is to block them off and treat them separately from the rest of the border. Run stripes up to the corner square and in that square repeat an image that was used elsewhere in the rug, as I did in Folk Art Stars.

- Miter the corners of striped borders. When you come to the corner in a border using random stripes, you can miter the corner and join the stripes. (See the illustration below.)

See how many border options you can come up with? The choices are endless and borders can be a lot of fun to plan. I think the best way to learn is by trial and error; you will find borders that really work with your style.

Finishing Your Rug

From binding techniques to blocking, signing, and caring for your rug, here are all the basics for finishing your rug.

Binding

If you are very careful in the binding of your rug, any of the following methods will be fine. Simply use the method you like best.

Whipstitched edges. Many people "whip" the edges of their rug, folding back the edges of the backing fabric and stitching them in place with woolen thread. The result is a very finished effect, but I find it time-consuming; perhaps because I don't like to sew!

Rug-binding tape. This method was used on most antique rugs, and it's a technique that I use frequently. It's faster than whipstitching the edges and makes a nice finish. It's also the most common finish on antique rugs, which is appealing to me. You can apply the binding tape to the backing in one of two ways.

Using a sewing machine, stitch the edge of the tape to the rug backing before you start to hook. That way you can hook right up to the sewn edge and have no backing fabric showing. The other way is to sew the binding on by hand after the rug has been hooked, sewing close to the edge of the rug and the tape. It's too hard to get close enough to the wool loops with a sewing machine once the rug has been hooked. Either way, the binding will finish off your rug nicely.

After hooking is completed, trim the backing fabric to about 1" all the way around the rug. Then fold the binding tape over the cut edge of the backing and hand sew the tape to the back of the rug.

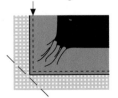

Stitch close to edge.

Trim corner to eliminate bulk.

Vintage fabric strips. I often bind my rugs with vintage fabric, as you will see on rugs in this book. Striped pillow ticking is my favorite. It's sturdy and adds a nice touch. To apply fabric, cut strips 1½" to 2" wide. Fold the strips in half lengthwise and then sew the raw edges of the fabric to the rug edges after the hooking is complete.

Wool strips. Another way to finish a rug is to use the strips of wool that you hooked into the rug. If you used large strips, such as a #9 cut, you may need to cut them in half so they are narrow enough to fit in a needle. Thread the wool strips into a large needle, such as a poultry trussing needle. Sew the edge of the rug to the back side with the wool strips.

Braiding. If you happen to be a rug braider, you can use that craft for finishing your hooked rugs, too. After hooking is complete, hand sew braided wool strips to the edge of the rug and then trim off the excess backing fabric. Rug braiding is a way to extend the size of your rugs, too. I don't braid, but I have hired a rug braider to add several inches of braiding to the perimeter of a rug in order to make a room-sized rug.

Blocking

Lay your hooked rug flat on a carpeted floor. If it's been pulled out of whack quite a bit, pull it as straight as you can and use long T-pins to secure it to the carpet. Wet a towel (or more than one for a large rug) and lay it over the rug. Using a steam iron, press the towel over the rug. Go over the entire surface until it is just slightly damp. Remove the towel and leave the rug to dry on the carpet overnight. You will have a straight rug.

RUG REPAIR KIT

My friend Patty Yoder offers this clever idea. She saves her extra cut and uncut wool pieces from a rug and places them in a plastic bag that she marks with the rug's name. If a rug needs a repair, the wool is readily available and easily identifiable.

Signing Your Rug

It is important to sign your rug. Most often, rug hookers will hook their initials and date into the corner of the rug or actually work them into the design in a clever way. If you want to sign your rugs on the top surface, here's how to do it: Using any color in your basket, hook your name or initials and the date wherever you'd like the information to appear in the design. This provides a holding line for the information. Then, as you near the completion of the rug, determine if the color you selected for the signature is the one you want to keep. If you want to change the color, pull out the holding-line color and replace it with a new one. This makes the task much easier than trying to hook the information later when the surrounding loops are in place.

Another way to document your rugs is to make a fabric label and hand sew it to the back of the rug. Today, this is how I sign all of my rugs, although unfortunately in the beginning of my career I did not sign my work. Include the name of your rug, the date you hooked it, and who you made it for. Then sign the label.

Most of my labels are made in the shape of a star. I use muslin for some, but if I use black rug binding, then I may use black fabric as the background for my star. When I use pillow ticking to bind the rug, I then like to incorporate that fabric into the label.

If you like to stitch by machine, you may want to embroider labels with your sewing machine as my friend Patty Yoder does. She sews beautifully and uses this talent for documenting all her rugs.

When it comes to labeling, my advice is twofold: Always sign your rugs, and be creative in finding a method that is uniquely suited to you and your style of rugs.

Caring for Your Rug

Hooked rugs are durable. History shows us that. Just consider all the hooked rugs and quilts that you have admired over the years. These time-proven arts are more than a feast for the eyes, they were made for use and for comfort. Taken care of properly, these pieces will be around for a long time.

The biggest enemy of hooked rugs is water, so don't wash them or get them wet. The colors can run, mix, and become dull. Keep that in mind before placing a rug near a sink or tub.

Hooked rugs do need to be kept clean, though. Sand or dirt left in the fibers can cause damage to the wool strips. The best way to clean a hooked rug is to regularly use an electric broom. Don't use a heavier vacuum cleaner because it can often lift the rug from the floor. You can also take the rugs outside and shake them. If a rug becomes stained, it's best to mix up mild soap flakes, sponge the suds onto the rug, and then brush off the surface. I find that brushing them off with a damp sponge will pick up animal hairs, too. A damp sponge doesn't hold enough water to make the colors run.

We have hooked rugs all over our house. With an Airedale in residence and seven grandkids who visit often, my rugs get a lot of use and they're more durable than most people imagine. I read in a book that told the story of the early cottage industry of hooking rugs in Massachusetts at the turn of the twentieth century, "Treat the rugs with the same care in which they were made." That seems to say it all.

RUG PATTERNS

Folk Art Stars
38" x 45½"
1 square = ½"
Enlarge this pattern 600%.

Nine of Hearts
23" x 23"
1 square = ¼"
Enlarge this pattern 350%.

Old West Side
34" x 47"
1 square = ½"
Enlarge this pattern 600%.

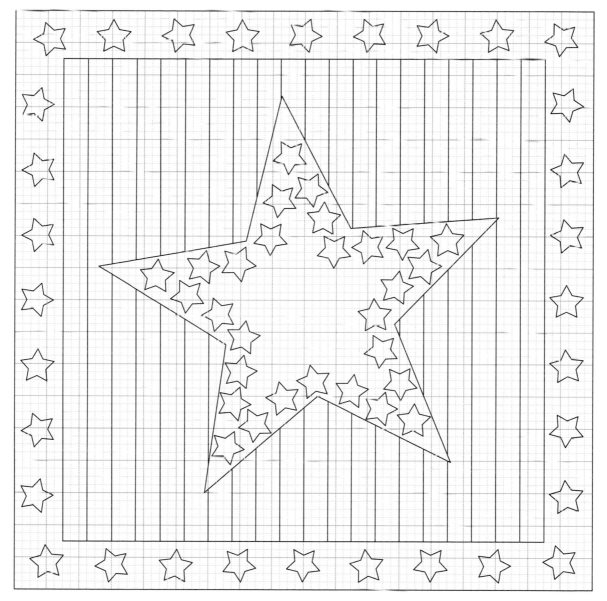

Stars on Stripes
36" x 36"
1 square = ½"
Enlarge this pattern 600%.

Airedale
33" x 22"
1 square = ½"
Enlarge this pattern 350%.

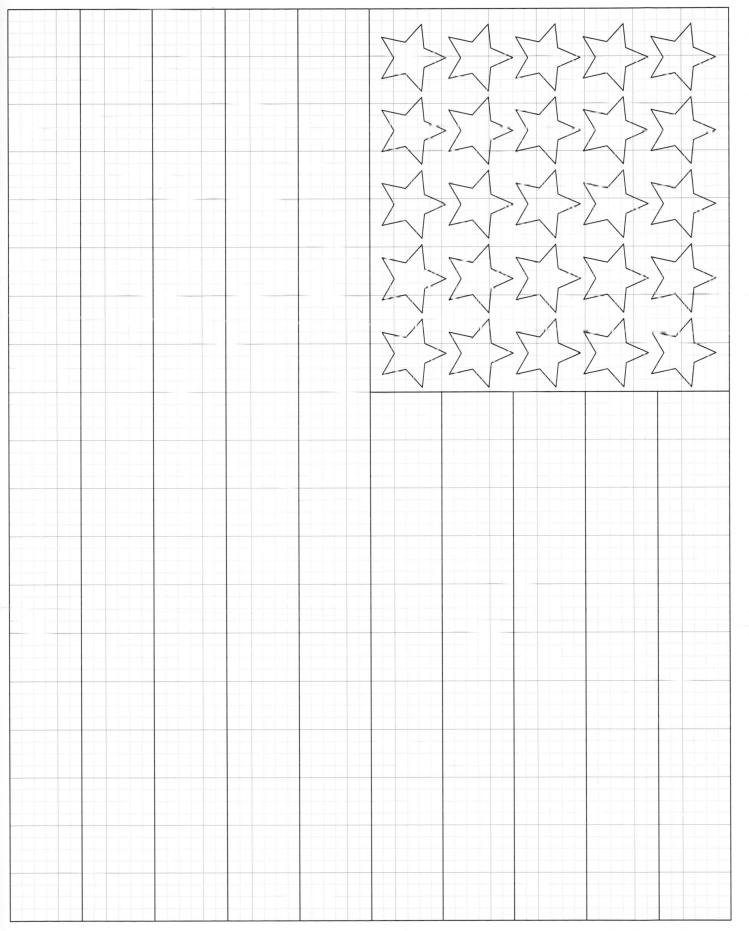

Star-Spangled Banner
38" x 30"
1 square = ½"
Enlarge this pattern 400%.

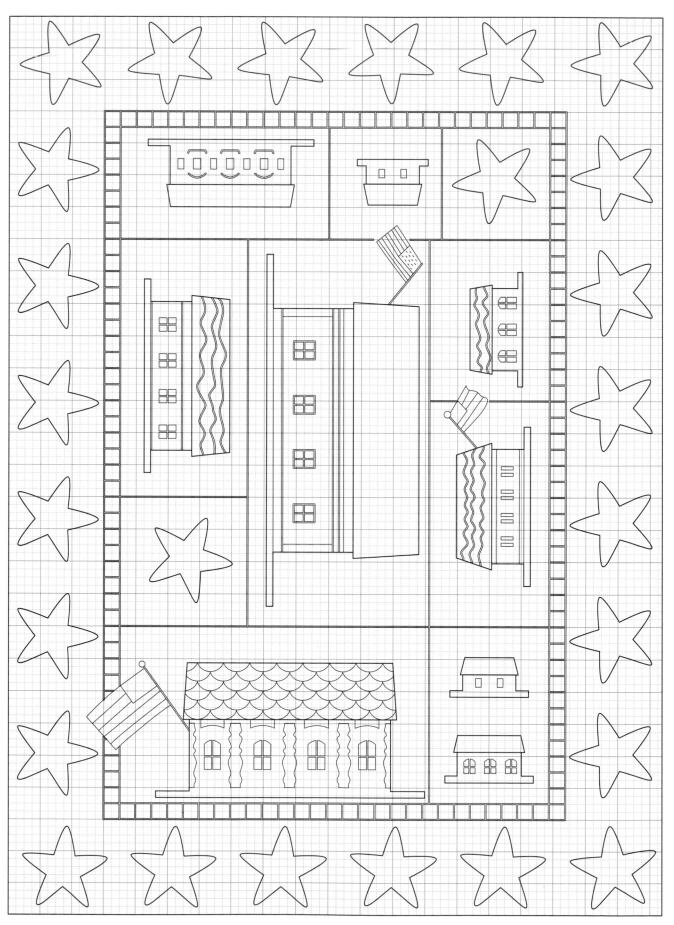

Noah's Ark
56" x 40¾"
1 square = ½"
Enlarge this pattern 600%.

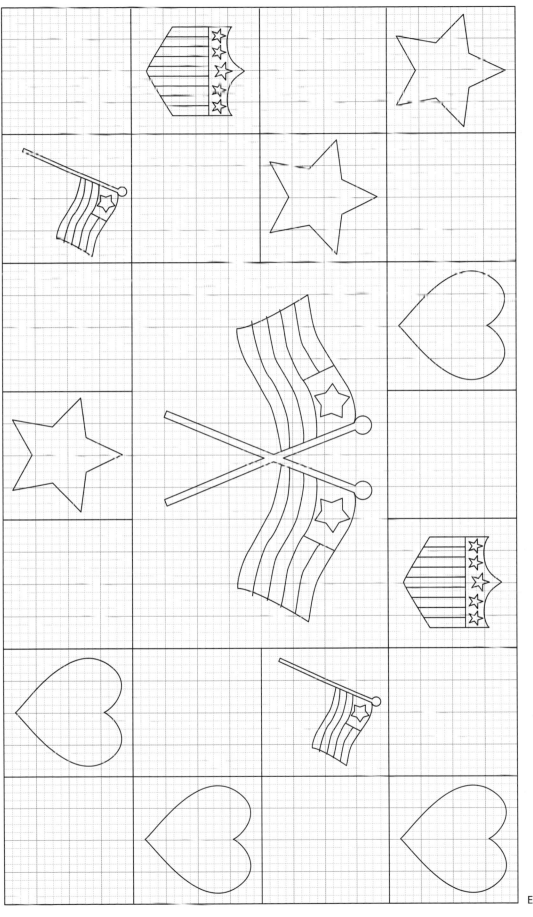

Make It Yours
56" x 32"
1 square = ½"
Enlarge this pattern 600%.

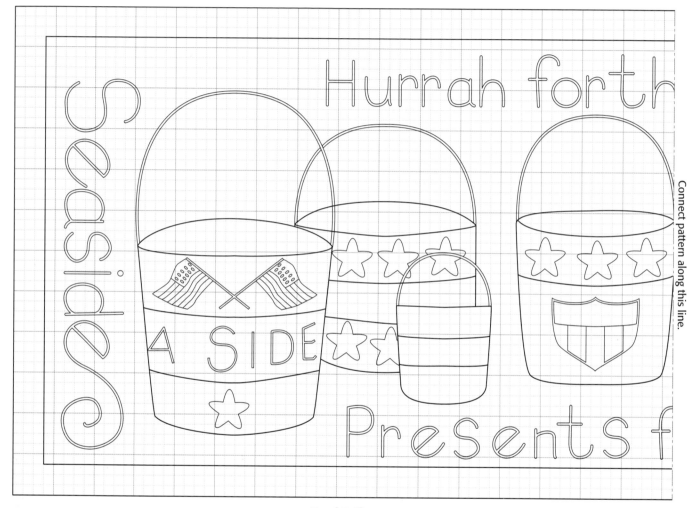

Sand Pails
65" x 24"
1 square = ½"
Enlarge this pattern 475%.

Sand Pails
65" x 24"
1 square = ½"
Enlarge this pattern 475%.

RESOURCES

For rug hooking equipment and supplies, check with your local fabric store, or contact one of the companies listed below.

Supplies

Braid Aid
PO Box 603, Route 53
Pembroke, MA 02359
(781) 826-6091
www.braid-aid.com
Various rug-hooking supplies, including hoops, hooks, wool, and more

Dorr Mill Store
PO Box 88
Guild, NH 03754
(800) 846-3677
www.dorrmillstore.com
Wool yardage, direct from the mill, as well as other hooking supplies

Drake's Wool
117 Windmill Point Road
White Stone, VA 22578
(804) 435-7100
www.drakeswool.com
Hand-dyed wool, rug backing, hoops and frames, cutters, and other supplies

Kindred Spirits
115 Colonial Lane
Kettering, OH 45429
(937) 435-7758
www.kindredspiritsdesigns.com
Hand-dyed wool, rug backing, hooks, hoops and frames, rotary-cutting system, and other supplies

The Wool Studio
Rebecca Erb
706 Brownsville Road
Sinking Spring, PA 19608
(610) 678-5448
www.thewoolstudio.com
Great source for "as-is" wool

Cutters

Harry M. Fraser Co.
PO Box 939
Stoneville, NC 27048
(336) 573-9830
www.fraserrugs.com
Fraser Model 500-1 and Bliss Cutting Machines

Rigby Precision Products
PO Box 158
Bridgton, ME 04009
(207) 647-5679
Rigby Cloth Stripping Machine

Townsend Industries, Inc.
Box 97
Altoona, IA 50009
(877) 868-3544
email: t-51info@t-51.com
Townsend Fabric Cutter

ACKNOWLEDGMENTS

Both Polly and Laurie would like to thank:

The entire staff of Martingale & Company for their continuing support and help, always there to answer any questions and give encouragement. A very special thanks!

The ladies of Little Quilts: Alice Berg, Mary Ellen Von Holt, and Sylvia Johnson, for their spirited support and guidance.

Rita Barnard for making the Heart penny rug, being a good friend, and helping out whenever asked.

Luanne Lea for her willingness to drop everything and hem a rug. Her beautiful sewing added so much to the project.

Mildred Moss for expert machine quilting.

In addition, Polly would like to personally thank:

My family: Jeff, John, and Jim along with Linda, Sharon, and Heidi for their continuing support and making me think, "I can do anything!" Thanks always.

Our special grandkids, Shelby, Grant, Rachel, Emily Kate, Thomas, Allison, and Michael, who are my constant inspiration and joy. You are the best!

My husband, Tom. A special thanks for always supporting and encouraging me, and for his willingness to help in any way. He is my most loyal supporter, my most honest critic, and a pretty good proofreader. Thanks!

Patty Yoder and Diane Kelly, my long-time hooking buddies who cheer me on when things are going well and endure me when I am struggling with a project. Thanks for always being there!

And Laurie, for saying "yes" when I called with this idea!

Laurie wishes to thank:

The Wednesday women who held my hand and cheered me on.

My family, Bill and Lorelei, who never doubted and always supported. A special thanks to Bill who got on his hands and knees to baste quilts.

And to Polly, for believing I could before I did.

About the Authors

Geraldine Mitchell

POLLY MINICK

Ann Keesor Photography

LAURIE SIMPSON

Polly and her husband of 40 years live on St. Simons Island in Coastal Southeast Georgia. The Minicks have three grown sons and seven grandchildren.

Polly began hooking rugs in 1984, and her rugs have met with praise from all, thanks to stories of her work in various national publications. Magazine articles in *Country Home, Better Homes and Gardens, Colonial Home, Coastal Living,* and *Victoria* have greatly expanded her audience. The *New York Times, Houston Chronicle,* and the *Georgetowner* have also written of Polly's achievements.

Like early-American rug hookers, Polly draws her inspiration from her love of home, family, nature, and country. Her patriotic works were inspired when one of her sons was commissioned an officer in the U.S. Marine Corps.

The ambiguity of Polly's motifs and patterns reflects her aim to preserve in the rugs her "naïve" quality. Her style is commonly described as "primitive, almost childlike," which places strong emphasis on her respect and solemn appreciation for early-American creations. Polly's imagery includes houses, horses, hearts, flags, stars, and birds, all of which reflect her love of family, country, and freedom.

Her enthusiasm and expertise as a collector of Americana and her national acclaim as a creator

of primitive-style hooked rugs have elevated Polly to being a guest lecturer. Various assemblies of fiber-artists guilds in Michigan, New York, North Carolina, Georgia, Vermont, and California have requested her commentary.

One of the benefits of authoring this book for Polly was the enjoyment of working with her sister, Laurie. In addition, she is excited about how the book will help promote fiber art as a true art and encourage others to follow her lead.

For over 30 years Laurie Simpson has delighted others with her quilts. Her work graces galleries and private collections and has been featured in *Country Home* and *Coastal Living* magazines. A patchwork quilt in a magazine inspired Laurie to take up quilting when she was 14. Drawn to traditional themes and techniques, she pieces, appliqués, and quilts exclusively by hand.

"I quilt in the car and at hockey games. Handwork is calming and meditative. It's the way I was meant to work," says Laurie.

Laurie lives with her husband, Bill, in Ann Arbor, Michigan. They share their home with a happy menagerie of four cats and a dog.